Pirates,
Puritans, and the
Perils of the High Seas

Further Titles Available from Psalm 78 Ministries

Ask of Me: John Paton, Missionary to the South Sea Cannibals, A History in Rhyme

Biblical Greek for Children

Biblical Hebrew for Children

Boundless in His Power: A History of God's working in Jamestown, as told by those who founded it

Driven to Resistance: A History of the Revolutionary War, as told by those who lived it

In Him Will I Trust: A Boy's Account of his Captivity among the American Indians

John Paton for Young Folks

The New England Primer: Essential Textbook of Christian Education

New Testament Greek for the Beginner

Pierre Viret: the Angel of the Reformation

Pierre Viret: Simple Exposition of the Christian Faith

Without a Home or Country: a Gallant Tale of the Last Stand of the Confederacy

Reformation Rhymes Series:

Volume One: They that Wait upon the Lord: Martin Luther and the Diet of Worms

Volume Two: God Shall Give the Increase: William Farel and the Reformation in Orbe

Volume Three: God Meant it unto Good: Pierre Viret and the Reformation in Switzerland and France

Volume Four: I Will Rejoice in the Lord: John Calvin and the Reformation in Geneva

For a full listing of available titles, please visit: www.psalm78ministries.com

Pirates, Puritans, and the Perils of the High Seas

Captain Charles Johnson
Puritan John Flavel
Edited by R. A. Sheats

Pirates, Puritans, and the Perils of the High Seas

Copyright © 2014 R. A. Sheats

All rights reserved.
No part of this publication may be reproduced or distributed in any form or by any means, without written consent from the publisher.

First printing, 2014

Published by:

Psalm 78 Ministries
P. O. Box 950
Monticello, FL 32345

www.psalm78ministries.com

ISBN: 978-1-938822-39-1

Printed in the United States of America.

Table of Contents

Seeking the Pirates' Treasure 9

Captain Avery

1 The Pirate Who Was Never Caught 13

2 The Trap is Sprung 25

Major Stede Bonnet

3 A Gentleman Turns Pirate 31

4 Strive to Enter in 41

Blackbeard

5 A Pirate's Reign of Terror 45

6 Save the Ship! 53

7 A Battle to the Death 57

8 Your Gold or Your Life? 67

The Dreaded Pirate Roberts

9 A Merry Life for Me! 71

10 The Deadliest Battle of All 81

11 Wine, Water, and Deserters 87

12 Sharks on Land 99

13 Deception and Death 105

14 Creatures from the Deep 117

Captain Anstis

15 A Divided Band of Pirates 125

16 The Leak that Sank the Ship 137

Captain Phillips and His Crew

17 Partners in Piracy 141

18 The Only Way of Escape 153

Introduction

Seeking the Pirates' Treasure

Nothing captivates the mind quite like a buried treasure. There's something so exciting, so enthralling, and so absolutely enchanting about a hidden cache of gold and silver, precious stones, and every wonder imaginable. For centuries men have sought out maps, diligently walked the paths, and relentlessly dug up thousands of acres of land, all in search of pirate treasure. After all the years that have passed and the multitude of treasure-seekers, is there any wealth left to be discovered? Is there *any* chance of unearthing more today?

Did pirates bury their treasure? And is it still there for the taking? In a word, yes. 300 years ago pirates lived in these lands. They walked our shores, they stalked our harbors, they sailed our seas. And their treasure remains to be found. *Pirates, Puritans, and the Perils of the High Seas* is an effort to unearth this vast treasure trove for the next generation.

What is the pirates' treasure? Gold and silver? Hardly. It's worth far more than that. What these desperate villains have left us is a hoard of incalculable wealth, of treasure beyond compare, but it must be sought ought, searched after, and hunted with diligence. Hard work is needed, 'tis true, but the reward far outweighs the effort. This treasure is worth more than rubies, and is valued higher than the finest gold:

> *Man knoweth not the price thereof; neither is it found in the land of the living. The depth saith, "It is not in me," and the sea saith, "It is not with me." It cannot be gotten for gold, neither shall silver be weighed for the price thereof. It cannot be valued with the gold of Ophir, with the precious onyx, or the sapphire. The gold and the crystal cannot equal it: and the exchange of it shall not be for jewels of fine gold.* (Job 28:13-17)

What is this treasure? Wisdom. "For wisdom is better than rubies; and all the things that may be desired are not to be compared to it" (Proverbs 8:11). Though centuries have passed since Blackbeard and his fellow-marauders plundered and murdered along these shores, yet the wisdom to be gleaned from their lives is still as fresh today as it was when the sound of their booming cannon filled the air.

But what is the wisdom to be gained from pirates? And what can be learned from studying them? Like all history, the lives of these desperadoes declare to us the glory of God, and are set forth for our instruction. After all, "the LORD hath made all things for Himself," even pirates, and He shall be glorified by them

(Proverbs 16:4).

One of the hidden gems in the history of the pirates is the revelation of the true nature of man. As Solomon stated, "Because sentence against an evil work is not executed speedily, therefore the heart of the sons of men is fully set in them to do evil" (Ecclesiastes 8:11). Pirates have a tendency to bring into crystal-clear focus the depravity of man and his consuming desire to be his own god.

The history of pirates also reveals to us the ways and workings of God. The psalmist declared, "I will remember the works of the LORD; surely I will remember Thy wonders of old" (Psalm 77:11). The stirring tales of eighteenth century piracy clearly display God's wondrous working with His creation, the necessity of His precious Law, and the unfathomable wonders of His never-failing grace.

A NOTE ON THE TEXTS

From the daring exploits of the dreaded pirate Roberts to the terrors of Blackbeard himself, the swash-buckling tales of pirates and piracy are here presented in a thrilling collection of the true stories of these desperate men. The accounts are written by Captain Charles Johnson, a man whose personal interviews with the pirates as well as his access to court records and other pertinent documents, lends life and accuracy to these exhilarating tales of pirates and those who hunted them.

Johnson's accounts appearing within this work have been taken from two of his works originally published under the titles *A General History of the Robberies and Murders of the Most Notorious Pirates*, and *The History of the Lives and Actions of the Most Famous Highwaymen, Street-Robbers, etc., etc., to which is Added a Genuine Account of the Voyages and Plunders of the Most Noted Pirates*. Johnson's narratives comprise every odd-numbered chapter within the present work.

As the Scriptures declare, wisdom is often difficult to locate, and it must be sought out by those who desire it. To assist in mining the wealth of wisdom from these piratical accounts, a selection of writings of the Puritan pastor John Flavel has been added to this history of the pirates. Flavel, born in 1628, grew up in an England filled with the horrifying exploits of the vast bands of pirates that then roved the seas. A minister for several years to a seaport congregation, Flavel had ample opportunity to observe and converse with the sailors and hardened seamen who frequented his town. With a desire to reach these men, Flavel published a work particularly written for sea-faring men entitled *Navigation Spiritualized, or A New Compass for Seamen*. Excerpts from Flavel's book have been interspersed throughout this volume, and appear in every even-numbered chapter.

Because both Captain Johnson and John Flavel penned their works over three hundred years ago, it has been deemed prudent to update various archaic words and phrases of the text and clarify highly-technical nautical terms. Certain words from the original have been left, and their definition given in footnotes. Chapter breaks and titles have been added, and Johnson's texts have also been abridged and purged of the more brutal aspects of piratical life.

Are you ready for a treasure hunt? Within the following pages, from the lives of the cunning pirate Avery and the bloodthirsty Roberts to the adventure-seeking Bonnet and the horrible Blackbeard, lies an incalculable wealth of wisdom. This is the treasure of the ages. This is the wealth awaiting us in the 'mines of history.'

Let us therefore "gird up the loins of our mind" and embark on a thrilling journey through the ages. Join the pirates and Puritans in this enthralling pursuit of the greatest treasure imaginable, while mining the depths of history and learning more and more of the Lord and "His wonderful works that He hath done" (Psalm 78:4).

R. A. Sheats

Captain Avery

Chapter One

The Pirate Who Was Never Caught

> *"For man also knoweth not his time:*
> *as the fishes that are taken in an evil net,*
> *and as the birds that are caught in the snare;*
> *so are the sons of men snared in an evil time,*
> *when it falleth suddenly upon them."*
>
> *— Ecclesiastes 9:12*

Captain Avery was born in the west of England, in Devonshire, and at an early period was sent to sea. He was advanced to the station of a mate in a merchantman,[1] as which he performed several voyages. He afterward served on a ship of thirty guns commanded by a Captain Gibson.

Avery was a fellow of more cunning than courage, and, gently and sneakily gaining the confidence of some of the boldest men in the ship (as well as the crew of another ship), he described to them the immense riches which were to be acquired upon the Spanish coast, and proposed to run off with the ship. The proposal was scarcely made when it was agreed upon, and carried out at ten o'clock the following evening.

---

[1] **merchantman** – a ship employed in trade

Captain Avery

Captain Gibson was one of those who mightily love their bottle, and spent much of his time on shore. But he remained aboard ship that night. This did not, however, frustrate Avery's plot, because Gibson had taken his usual dose, and so went to bed. The men who were not in the conspiracy went also to bed, leaving none upon deck but the conspirators.

At the time agreed upon, the longboat of the other ship came, which Avery hailed in the usual manner, and was answered by the men in her, "Is your drunken boatswain[2] on board?" which was the password agreed between them. After Avery

---

[2] **boatswain** – officer who superintends the sails, rigging, anchors, etc.

CAPTAIN GIBSON MIGHTILY LOVED HIS BOTTLE

replied in the affirmative, the boat came on board with sixteen stout fellows who joined in the adventure. They next secured the hatches, then softly weighed anchor and immediately put to sea without bustle or noise.

There were several vessels in the bay, and a Dutchman of forty guns, the captain of which was offered a considerable reward to go in pursuit of Avery, but he declined.

When Captain Gibson awoke, he felt the motion of the ship and rang his bell. Avery and another conspirator went into the cabin and found him yet half asleep. He questioned them, saying, "What is the matter with the ship?"

"Nothing," replied Avery.

"But something's the matter!" the captain exclaimed. "Is the anchor loose? What weather is it?" He supposed that it had been a storm, and that the ship was driven from her anchors.

"No, no," answered Avery. "We're at sea, with a fair wind and good weather."

"At sea!" exclaims the captain. "How can that be?"

"Come," says Avery, "don't be in a fright, but put on your clothes, and I'll let you into a secret. You must now know that I am captain of this ship, and this is *my* cabin. Therefore you must walk out. I am bound to Madagascar, with a design of making my own fortune and a fortune for all the brave fellows joined with me."

The Captain, having a little recovered his senses, began to understand the meaning of Avery's words. However, his terror was as great as before. Avery perceived this, and asked him to fear nothing. "For," says he, "if you have an inclination to join us, we will receive you. And if you turn sober and attend to business, perhaps in time I may make you one of my lieutenants. If not, here's a boat, and you shall be set on shore."

The Captain accepted of the last proposal. Then the whole crew was called up and asked who was willing to go on shore with the Captain. There were only about five or six who chose to accompany him.

Avery and his ship then proceeded on their voyage to Madagascar, and it does not appear that they captured any vessels upon their way. When they arrived at the northeast part of that island, they found two sloops[3] at anchor, who, upon seeing them, slipped their cables[4] and ran themselves ashore, while the men all landed and concealed themselves in the woods. These were two sloops which the men had stolen and run off with from the West Indies and, seeing Avery's ship, they supposed that he had been sent out after them.

Suspecting who they were, Avery sent some of his men on shore

---

[3] **sloops** – sailing vessels, generally having two masts

[4] **slipped their cables** – left quickly by leaving their cables without taking time to weigh the anchor

to inform them that they were friends, and to propose a union for their common safety.

The sloops' men were well-armed, and had posted themselves in a wood and placed sentinels on guard to observe whether the ship landed her men to pursue them. But when the sentinels only observed two or three men coming towards them unarmed, they did not oppose them. After being informed that they were friends, the sentinels brought Avery's men to the main body, where they delivered their message. They were at first afraid that it was a plot to trap them, but when the messengers assured them that their Captain had also run away with his ship, and that a few of their men along with him would meet them unarmed to discuss matters dealing with their mutual advantage, confidence was at last established. The men onshore were well pleased with the idea, as it added to their strength.

After Avery and the men had discussed what was most proper to be done, they endeavored to get the sloops out of the shallows, and hastened to prepare all things in order to sail for the Arabian coast.

Near the river Indus the man at the mast head spied a sail. They began a chase, and as they came nearer to her they discovered that she was a tall vessel, and might turn out to be an East Indiaman.[5] She, however, proved a better prize.[6] For, when they fired at her, she hoisted Mogul (or Mongolian) colors, and seemed to be preparing herself for defense.

Avery only cannonaded at a distance, when some of his men began to suspect that he was not the hero that they supposed. The sloops, however, attacked the ship, one on the bow,[7] and another upon the side of the ship, and so boarded her. She then lowered her flag and surrendered.

It turned out that she was a ship belonging to the great Mogul, the emperor of Mongolia, and there were in her several of the greatest persons in his court (among whom, it was said, was one of his daughters going upon a pilgrimage to Mecca), and they were carrying with them rich offerings to present at the shrine of Mohammed. It is a well-known fact that the people of the east travel with great magnificence, and these people had along with them all their slaves and attendants, with a large quantity of vessels of gold and silver, and immense sums of money to cover their expenses by land. Therefore the spoil which the pirates received from

---

[5] **East Indiaman** – a ship employed in transporting merchandise for the East India Company

[6] **prize** – vessel captured at sea

[7] **bow** – front (of a ship)

that ship was a wealth that could scarcely be measured.

The pirates took the treasure on board their own ships, plundered their prize of everything they wanted or liked, and then allowed her to depart. But, as soon as the Mogul received news of this, he threatened to send a mighty army to exterminate the English from all their settlements upon the Indian coast. The East India Company was greatly alarmed, but they managed to calm the Mogul's resentment by promising to search for the robbers and deliver them into his hands.

In the meantime our adventurers made the best of their way back to Madagascar. They intended to make that place the deposit of all their treasure, to build a small fort there, and to always keep a few men there for its protection. Avery, however, interrupted this plan, and made it altogether unnecessary.

While steering their course, Avery sent a boat to each of the sloops,

requesting that the chiefs would come on board his ship to hold a conference. They obeyed and, being assembled, he suggested to them the necessity of making their newly-gotten wealth secure in some safe place on shore. He explained that the main difficulty was to get it safe on shore, because, if any of the sloops happened to be attacked alone, they would not be able to make any great resistance, and thus they would either be sunk or captured, with all the treasure on board.

To solve this problem, Avery declared that his vessel was so strong, so well-manned, and such a swift-sailing vessel that he did not think that it was possible for any other ship to catch or overcome her. Accordingly, he proposed that all their treasure should be sealed up in three chests—that each of the captains should have keys, and that they should not be opened until all were present—and that the chests should then be put on board his own ship, and afterwards secured in some safe place on land.

This proposal seemed so reasonable and so beneficial for the common good, that it was accordingly agreed to, and all the treasure was deposited in three chests and carried to Avery's ship.

The weather continued favorable, and all three vessels remained in company during that and the next day. Meanwhile Avery, secretly speaking with his men, suggested that, now that they had on board a treasure sufficient to make them all happy, he asked, "What now hinders us from going to some country where we are not known, and living onshore all the rest of our days in wealth and luxury?"

Avery's crew soon understood his hint, and all eagerly agreed to deceive the men of the sloops, and to slip away with all the booty. They managed to carry this off during the darkness of the following night. The reader may easily imagine the feelings and indignation of the other two crews in the morning, when they discovered that Avery had made off with all their property.

Avery and his men hastened

SECURING THE TREASURE CHESTS

towards America and, being strangers in that country, they agreed to divide their booty, to change their names, and separately to take up their residence and live in abundance of riches and honor.

The first land they approached was at the island of Providence, then newly settled. It however occurred to them that the largeness of their vessel would cause quite a stir, and the report that one had been stolen might create suspicion. Therefore they resolved to dispose of their vessel at Providence.

Upon this resolution Avery entered the port, pretending that his vessel had been equipped for privateering[8] and, having been unsuccessful, he had orders from the owners to dispose of her to the best advantage. Under this disguise he soon found a merchant interested in purchasing the vessel. Having thus sold his own ship, he immediately purchased a small sloop.

In this vessel he and his companions embarked, and landed at several places in America where, none suspecting them, they dispersed and settled in the country. Avery, however, had been careful to conceal the greater part of the jewels and other valuable articles, so that his riches were immense. Arriving at Boston, he was almost resolved to settle there, but as the greater part of his wealth consisted of diamonds, he was afraid that he could not dispose of them at that place without being arrested as a pirate.

Upon consideration, therefore, he decided to sail for Ireland, and in a short time arrived in the northern part of that kingdom, and his men dispersed into different places.

The wealth of Avery, however, now proved of very little use to him and caused him great uneasiness. He could not offer his diamonds for sale in that country without being suspected. Considering, therefore, what was best to be done, he thought there might be some person at Bristol he could dare to trust. After he had decided upon this he went into Devonshire, and sent to one of his friends to meet him at a town

---

[8] **privateering** – the act of cruising against an enemy in a private sailing vessel

called Biddiford.

When Avery had revealed his secret to his aquaintance and other supposed friends, they agreed that the safest plan would be to put his jewels into the hands of some wealthy merchants, and no inquiry would be made how they came by them.

One of these friends told him that he was acquainted with some merchants who were very fit for the purpose, and if Avery would allow them a handsome commission, they would do the business faithfully. Avery liked the idea, particularly as he could think of no other way of managing this matter, since he could not appear to act for himself. Accordingly the merchants paid Avery a visit at Biddiford, where, after strong declarations of honor and integrity, he delivered to them his treasure, consisting of diamonds and some vessels of gold. After giving him a little money for his present needs, the merchants departed.

Avery then changed his name and lived very quietly at Biddiford; therefore there was no notice taken of him. In a short time, however, his money was all spent, yet he heard no word from his merchants. He wrote them repeatedly, and at last they sent him a small supply of money, but it was not sufficient to pay his debts. In short, the payments they sent him were so trifling that it was with great difficulty that he could even exist. He therefore determined to go privately to Bristol and have an interview with the merchants himself.

But when he visited them, instead of money, he met with a humiliating rejection. For, when he demanded them to come to an account with him, they silenced him by threatening to reveal his true character. (Thus the merchants proved themselves to be as good pirates at land as Avery was at sea.)

Whether Avery was frightened by these threats or whether he had seen some other person who recognized him, is not known. However, he went immediately to Ireland, and from there desperately pleaded with his merchants for a supply, but it did no good. Soon he was reduced to beggary.

In this extreme distress he was determined to return and throw himself upon the mercy of these "honest" Bristol merchants, let the consequence be what it would. He therefore went on board a trading vessel and worked his passage over to Plymouth. From there he traveled on foot to Biddiford. But he had been there only a few days when he fell sick and died, not even having enough money to buy himself a coffin.

> *"For man also knoweth not his time:*
> *as the fishes that are taken in an evil net,*
> *and as the birds that are caught in the snare;*
> *so are the sons of men snared in an evil time,*
> *when it falleth suddenly upon them."*
>
> — *Ecclesiastes 9:12*

Chapter Two

The Trap is Sprung

While you by skill the silly fish do kill,
Perhaps the devil's hook sticks in your *gill.*

There is skill in fishing. They that go to sea on a fishing voyage are accustomed to go provided with their *craft* (as they very fitly call it) without which they can do nothing. They have their lines, hooks of several sizes, and their bait. They carefully observe their seasons, and when the fish come in, then they steadily labor at their business day and night.

Application

But how much more skilful and industrious is Satan to ensnare and destroy souls? The devil makes a voyage as well as you. He has his baits for you just as you have for the fish. He has his traps and snares to catch souls (2 Corinthians 2:11; Ephesians 6:11). He is a serpent, an old serpent (Revelation 12:9). Too cunning and deceptive for man in his state of perfection, how much more easily shall he entrap us in our collapsed and degenerate state, now that our mind is cracked by the fall, and all our understanding is poisoned and perverted!

Ministers observe four steps or degrees of Satan's tempting power:

First, he can find out the evils that best suit a man's frame of mind. He knows to what sins their natures are more especially prone to, and inclinable.

Secondly, he can offer and set forth suitable objects to those lusts. He can exactly and fully make use of every man's desire in order to more easily entice him to sin.

Thirdly, he can inject and cast ideas and desires into the mind, urging man to unite with those tempting objects. As it is said of Judas, the devil put it into his heart to betray Christ (John 13:2).

Fourthly, he can disturb, irritate, and provoke the heart, and by those continual disturbances and invitations, weary it. And by this he often induces men to commit such things as startled them when the idea first presented itself to their minds.

All this he can do, if he finds the work sticks and meets with rubs and difficulties; yet he does not act to the utmost of his skill and power at all times and with all persons; neither indeed need he do so. The very setting forth and revealing of an object is enough to some, without any further suggestions; the devil makes an easy conquest of them.

And, besides all this, he is very clever in choosing when, where, and by whom he introduces his temptations, and by this poor souls are caught, as fish in an evil net (Ecclesiastes 9:12).

The carnal man is led by sense, as the beast; and Satan handles and fits him accordingly. He uses all sorts of motives, not only internal and mental, but external and sensitive also; as the sparkling of the wine, when it gives its color in the glass, or the harlot's beauty, whose eye-lids are snares, hiding always the hook, and concealing the issue from them. He promises man gain and profit, pleasure and delight, and all that is tempting, with assurance of secrecy. By these he fastens the fatal hook in their jaws, and thus they are led captive by him at his will.

REFLECTION

And is Satan so subtle and diligent to entice souls to sin? Does he thus cast out his golden baits and allure souls with pleasure to their ruin? Then how necessary is it for you, O my soul, to be careful and wary! How strict a guard should I set upon every sense! Ah, let me not so much regard how sin comes towards me in the temptation, as how it goes off at last. The day in which Sodom was destroyed began with a pleasant sun-shine, but ended in fire and brimstone. I may promise myself much happiness in the fulfillment of my lusts, but O how certainly will it end in my ruin!

Ahab doubtless promised himself much satisfaction in the vineyard of Naboth, but his blood paid for it in the portion of Jezreel. The harlot's bed was perfumed to tempt the simple young man (Proverbs 7:17). But those chambers of delights proved to be the chambers of death, and her house the way to hell.

Ah, with what a smiling face sin comes on towards me in its temptations! How it tickles the carnal desires and pleases the deceived heart! But what a dreadful catastrophe and end it has! The delight is quickly gone, but its guilt remains to horrify and terrify the soul with ghastly images and dreadful pictures of the wrath of God! Just as sin has its delights accompanying it to enter and fasten it, so it has its horrors and stings to torment and wound. And as certainly as I see those go before it to make a way, so certainly shall I find these follow after, and tread upon its heels. No sooner is the conscience awakened, but all those delights vanish as a night vision, or as a dream when one awakes: and then I shall cry:

"Here is the hook, but where is the bait? Here is the guilt and horror, but where is the pleasure and delight that I was promised? And I, where shall I now go? Ah, my deceitful lusts! You have enticed and left me in the midst of all miseries!"

The Trap is Sprung

There's skill in fishing—that the devil knows,
For when for souls Satan a-fishing goes,
He fishes cunningly. He knows he must
Exactly fit the bait unto the lust.

He studies man's affections, place, and time,
He guesses what is his delight, what thine,
And so accordingly prepares the bait
While he himself lies closely hid, to wait,

To see when you'll latch on. Are you inclined
To drunken meetings? Then he baits with wine:
Is this the way? If unto this he'll smell,
He'll shortly pledge a cup of wrath in hell.

To pride or lust is your vile nature bent?
An object suitable he will present.
O think on this, when you cast in the hook:
Say, "Thus for my poor soul doth Satan look."

O play not with temptations, do not swallow
The sugared bait—consider what will follow!
If once he catch thee, then away he draws
Thy captive soul, a pris'ner in his paws.

Major Stede Bonnet

Major Stede Bonnet

Chapter Three

A Gentleman Turns Pirate

*"Today, if ye will hear His voice,
harden not your hearts."*

— *Hebrews 4:7*

Major Stede Bonnet (before he became a pirate) was a gentleman of a considerable fortune in the island of Barbados. It was therefore surprising that he should embark in such a dishonorable and dangerous undertaking as piracy. Having formed his resolution, however, he equipped a small vessel of ten guns and seventy men at his own expense, and in the dead of night commenced his voyage.

In this vessel, named the *Revenge,* he sailed for the Cape of Virginia, where he captured several vessels which he plundered. After several good prizes, he directed his course to Long Island, where he took a sloop[1] bound for the West Indies, and then landed some men at Gardner's Island, paid for whatever provisions were necessary, and left without doing any injury. His next adventure was the capturing of two other vessels.

The Major found no small difficulty in reconciling the different opinions

---

[1] **sloop** – sailing vessel, generally having two masts

of his crew on what course they should next steer. Because he was himself no sailor, he was frequently under the necessity of yielding to the foolish opinion of others. He at last found an accomplished fellow-helper in Edward Teach, commonly called Blackbeard. To him the Major's crew united their fortunes, while Stede Bonnet himself went on board Teach's ship and remained as a private sailor.

In this situation Bonnet soon began to reflect upon his past life, and was filled with remorse and shame because of his evil conduct. This change in his mindset was discovered by his companions, and he made known his burning desire to retire into some foreign country to spend the remainder of his days in solitude.

About this time Bonnet, Blackbeard, and the numerous other pirates became such a plague to England that the king and parliament realized that something drastic must be done to put a stop to the murder and theft so rampant on the high seas. The king at last decided to issue a pardon to all pirates who would leave their piratical profession and promise to return to a lawful occupation. The decree was issued in September of 1716, and declared pardon for all pirates who surrendered prior to September 5, 1717.

Blackbeard some time after surrendered to the royal proclamation of the king, and obtained pardon. The Major then assumed the command of his own ship, immediately sailed to Bath Town in North Carolina, and likewise surrendered to his Majesty's proclamation.

Upon his return, Bonnet found that Blackbeard had betrayed him and had

plundered the great ships of money and arms, and marooned seventeen of the crew in a deserted island. Being informed of this by two who had escaped, Bonnet sent the longboat to the crew's assistance, so that, after remaining two days without food, and in the prospect of a lingering death, the men were all taken on board the Major's ships.

Bonnet then informed his men that his intention was to take a commission to prey against the Spaniards, and that he would take them along with him if they were inclined. To this they all readily agreed.

Just, however, as they were about to sail, they received information that Blackbeard was not far off, with only eighteen or twenty men. The Major pursued him, but was too late to catch him. Disappointed in their pursuit, they instead directed their course to Virginia.

When off the Capes they met a vessel, out of which they took twelve barrels of pork and four hundred weight of bread and, in return, gave them eight or ten casks of rice and an old cable. Two days after he captured a vessel off Cape Henry, in which were several casks of rum and other articles of which they stood greatly in want.

Under the name of Captain Thomas, Major Bonnet suddenly resumed his former piratical raids. Off Cape Henry he took two ships bound from Virginia to Glasgow, which only supplied them with some hundreds weight of tobacco. The following day he seized one bound to Bermuda, which supplied him with twenty barrels of pork. And, in return, he gave her two barrels of rice and a hogshead[2] of molasses. From this ship two men entered into their service.

The next prize was a ship from Virginia bound for Glasgow, from which they received nothing of value. In the course of their cruising several vessels were captured, though of no considerable value.

Our pirates next sailed for Cape

---

[2] **hogshead** – large barrel

Fier river, where they waited too long, because their vessel proved leaky, and they could not proceed until she was refitted. Meanwhile, the Council of South Carolina received information that a pirate was discovered with her prizes at no great distance. At this the council was alarmed, and two vessels under Colonel Rhet were equipped and sent in search of the pirates.

After a considerable search they were discovered. Rhet, arriving with his two sloops at the river where Major Bonnet and his prizes[3] lay, directed his course up the river to attack the pirates as the sun began to set. But it happened that in going up the river the pilot ran the colonel's sloops aground, and it was dark before they were afloat, which prevented their catching up to the pirates that night.

The pirates soon discovered the sloops but, not knowing who they were or why they came into that river, they manned three canoes and sent them down to take them. But the men quickly discovered their mistake, and returned to Bonnet with the unwelcome news.

Major Bonnet made preparations that night for a battle with the sloops, and took all the men out of the prizes. He showed Captain Manwaring, one of his prisoners, a letter he had just written, which he declared he would send to the Governor of Carolina. The letter declared that, if the sloops which then appeared in the river were sent out against him by the governor, and if Bonnet should escape from them, then he would burn and destroy all ships or vessels going into or coming out of South Carolina.

---

[3] **prizes** – vessels captured at sea

The next morning the pirates got under sail and came down the river with the intention of slipping past the sloops while firing upon them. Colonel Rhet's sloops also got under sail, and closed in on either side of the pirate. A severe battle ensued, and Bonnet and his crew were made prisoners.

The Colonel took possession of the pirate sloop, and was extremely pleased to find that "Captain Thomas," the pirate who commanded her, was none other than Major Stede Bonnet, who had done them the honor several times of visiting their own coast of Carolina.

Colonel Rhet brought the pirates ashore and placed them in the guard house under a guard of militia, until the men could be brought to trial. In a short time, however, Major Bonnet and one other pirate, Hariot, made their escape. This greatly alarmed the inhabitants, who feared that Bonnet would again find means to get a vessel and wreak his vengeance upon them.

The governor, upon hearing of the escape, offered a reward of seven hundred pounds for Bonnet's capture, and sent Colonel Rhet in pursuit of him. Therefore the colonel sailed away that night to Sullivan's Island and, after a very diligent search, discovered Bonnet and Hariot together. The colonel's men fired upon them and killed Hariot upon the spot, but the Major surrendered and was brought to Charleston for trial.

Appearing before the court, Bonnet was tried, found guilty, and received the sentence of death. Judge Trot pronounced the sentence of death upon the prisoner, but first exhorted him with the following most good and useful words:

"Major Stede Bonnet, you stand here convicted upon two indictments of Piracy: one by the verdict of the jury, and the other by your own confession.

"You know that the crimes you have committed are evil in themselves, and contrary to the light and law of nature, as well as the Law of God, by which you are commanded that you should not steal (Exodus 20:15). And the Apostle Paul expressly affirms that thieves shall not inherit the Kingdom of God (1 Corinthians 6:10).

"But to theft you have added a greater sin, which is murder. How many you may have killed of those that resisted you in the committing of your former piracies, I know not. But this we all know, that besides the wounded, you killed no less than eighteen persons out of those that were sent by lawful authority to suppress you, and to put a stop to those acts of plundering and violence that you daily committed.

"And, though you may suppose that this was killing men fairly in open fight, yet know this, that as the power of the Sword was not committed into your hands by any lawful authority, you were not empowered to use any force or to fight any one. And therefore those persons that fell in that battle, while doing their duty to their king and country, were murdered, and their blood now cries out for vengeance and justice against you. For it is the voice of nature, confirmed by the Law of God, that "whoso sheddeth man's blood, by man shall his blood be shed" (Genesis 9:6).

"And consider that death is not the only punishment due to murderers, for they are declared to have their part in the lake which burns with fire and brimstone, which is the second death (Revelation 21:8, 22:15). These are words which carry that terror with them that, considering your circumstances and your guilt, surely the sound of them must make you tremble. For who can dwell with everlasting burnings? (Isaiah 33:14.)

"As the testimony of your conscience must convince you of the great and many evils you have committed, by which you have highly offended God and provoked most justly His wrath and indignation against you, so I suppose I need not tell you that the only way of obtaining pardon and remission of your sins from God is by a true and sincere repentance and faith in Christ, by whose meritorious death and passion you can only hope for salvation.

"You being a gentleman that has had the advantage of a good education, and being generally esteemed a man of learning, I believe it will be needless for me to explain to you the nature of repentance and faith in Christ, they being so fully and so often mentioned in the Scriptures, that you cannot but know them. And therefore, perhaps, it might be thought by some improper for me to have said so much to you as I have already said upon this occasion. Neither should I have done it, but that, considering the course of your life and actions, I have good reason to fear that the principles of religion that were instilled into you by your education have been at least corrupted, if not entirely defaced, by the skepticism and unbelief of this wicked Age.

"Had your delight been in the Law of the Lord, and had you meditated therein day and night (Psalm 1:1-2), you would then have found that God's Word was a Lamp unto your feet and a Light to your path (Psalm 119:105). You would then count all other knowledge but loss, in comparison of the excellency of the knowledge of Christ Jesus (Philippians 3:8), who to them that are called is the Power of God, and the Wisdom of God (1 Corinthians 1:24). He is even the hidden Wisdom which God ordained before the foundation of the world (1 Corinthians 2:7).

"You would then have esteemed the Scriptures as the Great Charter of Heaven, and which deliver to us not only the most perfect Laws and Rules of Life, but also revealed to us those Acts of Pardon from God, in which we have offended those righteous Laws. For in them only is to be found the great mystery of fallen man's redemption, which the angels desire to look into (1 Peter 1:12).

"The Scriptures also would have taught you that sin is the debasing of human nature, it being a turning away from that purity, righteousness, and holiness in which God created us. They teach us that virtue and religion, and walking by the Laws of God, are altogether preferable to the ways of sin and Satan, for the ways of virtue are ways of pleasantness, and all her paths are peace (Proverbs 3:17).

"But what you have not learned from God's Word because of your carelessness, or your lightly considering the same, I hope the way of His Providence, and the present afflictions that He has laid upon you, have now convinced you of the same. For, though in your prosperity you might make a mock at your sins (Proverbs

3:17), yet, now that you see that God's Hand has reached you and brought you to public justice, I hope your present unhappy circumstances have made you seriously consider your past actions and way of life, and that you are now sensible of the greatness of your sins, and that you find the burden of them is intolerable.

"Therefore, being thus laboring and heavy-laden with sin (Matthew 5:28), may you make it your greatest endeavor to seek the knowledge which will show you how you can be reconciled to that supreme God whom you have so highly offended. Seek Him who can reveal to you Himself, who is not only the powerful Advocate with the Father for you (1 John 2:1), but is He who has also paid that debt which is due for your sins by His own death upon the cross. He has made full satisfaction to the Justice of God.

"And this knowledge is to be found nowhere but in God's Word, which reveals to us that Lamb of God which taketh away the sins of the world (John 1:29), who is Christ, the Son of God. For know and be assured that there is *none other Name* under Heaven given among men, whereby we must be saved (Acts 4:12).

"But then consider how He invites all sinners to come unto Him, and that He will give them rest (Matthew 11:28). For He assures us that He came to seek and to save that which was lost (Luke 19:10; Matthew 18:11), and has promised that whoever comes unto Him, He will in no wise cast out (John 6:37).

"So that if now you will sincerely turn to Him, though late—even at the eleventh hour (Matthew 20:6, 9)—He will receive you.

"But surely I need not tell you that the terms of His mercy are faith and repentance.

"And do not mistake the nature of repentance to be only a bare sorrow for your sins, arising from the consideration of the evil and punishment they have now brought upon you. But your sorrow must arise from the consideration of your having offended a gracious and merciful God.

"But I shall not endeavor to give you any particular directions as to the nature of repentance, for I know that I speak to a person whose offenses have not proceeded from his ignorance as much as from his despising and neglecting his duty.

"I only heartily wish that what, in compassion to your soul, I have now said to you upon this sad and solemn occasion, may have that due effect upon you so that you may become truly repentant.

"And, therefore, having now discharged my duty to you as a Christian (by giving you the best counsel I can with respect to the salvation of your soul), I must now do my office as a Judge.

"The sentence that the law has appointed to pass upon you for your offenses, and which this Court does therefore award, is:

"That you, Stede Bonnet, shall go from hence to the place from which you came, and from thence to the Place of Execution, where you shall be hanged by the neck till you are dead. And may the God of infinite mercy be merciful to your soul."

"Today, if ye will hear His voice,
harden not your hearts."

— *Hebrews 4:7*

EXECUTION DOCK

Chapter Four

Strive to Enter in

If seamen lose a gale, there they must lie.
The soul, when once becalmed in sin, may die.

Seamen are very watchful to take their opportunity of wind and tide, and it is their great concern to be so. The neglect of a few hours, sometimes, loses them their passage, and proves a great loss to them. They know the wind is an uncertain, changeable thing. They must take it when it offers itself. They are unwilling to lose one flow or breath that may be serviceable to them. If a prosperous gale offers itself and they are not ready, it sorrows them to lose it, as much as it would sorrow us to see a vessel of good wine pierced through and run to waste.

Application

There are also seasons and winds of grace for our souls, golden opportunities of salvation offered to men, and the neglect of these proves the loss and ruin of souls. God has given unto man a day of visitation, which He has limited (Hebrews 4:7). And He keeps an exact account of every year, month, and day that we have enjoyed it (Luke 13:7, 19:42; Jeremiah 25:3). The longest date of it can only be the length of the time of this life. This is our day to work in (Job 9:4), and upon this small wire the weight of eternity hangs.

But sometimes the season of grace is ended before the night of death comes. The accepted time is gone; men frequently outlive it (Luke 19:44; 2 Corinthians 6:2). Or, if the outward means of salvation be continued, yet the Spirit many times withdraws from those means, and ceases any more to strive with men. And then the blessing, power, and effectiveness is gone from them, and instead of these a curse seizes the soul (Hebrews 6:7-8; Jeremiah 6:29).

Therefore it is a matter of utmost importance to our souls to take hold of these seasons. How passionately Christ bewails Jerusalem upon this account! "O that thou hadst known, at least in this thy day, the things of thy peace! But now they are hid from thine eyes!" (Luke 19:42.)

If a company of seamen are set ashore upon some remote, uninhabited island, with this advice: "Be here again at exactly such an hour, or else you shall be left behind," how greatly concerned will they be to be punctual to their time? The

lives of those men depend upon a quarter of an hour. Many a soul has perished eternally (the Gospel leaving them behind in their sins) because they knew not the time of their visitation.

REFLECTION

What golden seasons for salvations have you enjoyed, O my soul! What peaceful, happy days of Gospel-light and grace have you had? How have the precious winds of grace blown to no purpose upon you! And has the Spirit waited and striven with you in vain? The Kingdom of Heaven (being opened in the times of the Gospel) has suffered violence (Matthew 11:12). Multitudes have been pressing into it in my days, and I myself have sometimes been almost persuaded, and not far from the kingdom of God. I have gone as far as conviction of sin and misery. Yes, I have been carried by the power of the Gospel, to resolve and purpose to turn to God and become a new creature; but sin has been too subtle and deceitful for me. I see my resolutions were but as an early cloud or morning dew; and now my heart is cold and dead again, settled upon its lees. Ah! I have cause to fear and tremble, lest God has left me under that curse: "Let him that is filthy, be filthy still" (Revelation 20:11).

I fear I am become as that miry place (Ezekiel 47:11) that shall not be healed by the streams of the Gospel, but given to salt, and cursed into perpetual barrenness. Ah Lord! Will You leave me so? And shall Your Spirit strive no more with me? Then it had been better for me that I had never been born. Ah! If I have stifled out this season, and forever lost it, then I may take up that lamentation, and say, "My harvest is past, my summer is ended, and I am not saved" (Jeremiah 8:20).

Every creature knows its time. Even the turtledove, crane, and swallow know the time of their coming (Jeremiah 8:7). How beastly am I that have not known the time of my visitation! O, You are the Lord of life and time! Permit me one gracious season more, and make it effective to me, before I go from here, and be seen no more!

A fresh and blowing wind is here today,
But now the ship's not ready; winds must stay
And wait the seamen's leisure. Well, tomorrow
They will put out. But then, unto their sorrow,

That wind is spent, and by that means they gain
Perhaps a month of waiting, if not twain.[1]
At last another offers. Now they're gone,
But ere[2] they gain their port, the market's done.

For ev'ry work and purpose under heav'n,
A proper time and season God has giv'n.
The fowls of heaven, swallow, dove, and crane,
Do understand it, and put us to shame.

Man has his season, too, but that misspent,
There's time enough his folly to repent.
Eternity's before him, but therein
No more such golden hours as these have been.
When these are passed away, then you shall find
That it's now far too late to look behind.

Delays are dang'rous. See that you discern
Your proper seasons. O! that you would learn
This wisdom from these fools who come too late
With fruitless cries, when Christ has shut the gate.

*"Strive to enter in at the strait gate: for many,
I say unto you, will seek to enter in,
and shall not be able."*

— *Luke 13:24*

---

[1] **twain** – two

[2] **ere** – before

Blackbeard

Chapter Five

A Pirate's Reign of Terror

"It is as sport to a fool to do mischief."

— *Proverbs 10:23*

Edward Teach was born in Bristol, but had sailed some time out of Jamaica in privateers in the late French war. Yet, though he had often distinguished himself for his uncommon boldness and personal courage, he was never raised to any command till he went a-pirating, which I think was at the latter end of the year 1716.

Now *Thatch* or *Teach* was the real name of this bloody desperado, but he was better known by his piratical name Blackbeard. He received this name from the large quantity of hair which, like a frightful meteor, covered his whole face and frightened America more than any comet that has appeared there a long time.

His beard was black, and he allowed it to grow to an extravagant length. As to breadth, it came up to his eyes. He was accustomed to twist it with ribbons in small twists, resembling those of some fashionable wigs, and turn them about his ears. In time of battle he wore a sling over his shoulders, with three pairs of pistols hanging in holsters. He wore a fur cap, and stuck a lighted match on each side under it, which, appearing on each side of his face (his eyes naturally looking fierce and wild), made him altogether such a figure that imagination cannot form an idea

of a demon from hell to look more frightful.

If Blackbeard had the look of a demon, his tempers and passions were suitable to it. We shall relate two or three of his wild and beastly actions, by which it will appear to what a depth of wickedness human nature may arrive if its passions are not restrained.

When Teach began his piratical career, he mounted his vessel with forty guns and named her *The Queen Anne's Revenge*. Cruising near the island of St. Vincent, he took a large ship called the *Great Allan* and, after having plundered her of what he wanted, he set her on fire.

A few days afterward Teach met with a man-of-war[1] and battled her for some hours. But when the man-of-war saw his strength and determination, she retired and left Teach to pursue his plundering and violence.

His next adventure was with a sloop of ten guns commanded by Major Bonnet (whose actions we have already described). These two pirates united their fortunes and co-operated for some time. But Teach found Bonnet ignorant of naval affairs, and gave the command of Bonnet's ship to Richards, one of his own crew, and gave Bonnet lodgings on board of his own vessel.

Watering at Turniff, they discovered a sail, and Richards with the *Revenge* slipped her cable[2] and ran out to meet her. Upon seeing the black flag hoisted, the vessel immediately surrendered, and came to under the stern of Teach the commodore. This was the *Adventure* from Jamaica. They took the captain and his men on board the great ship, and took his sloop for their own service.

The pirates weighed anchor from Turniff, where they remained during a week and, sailing to the Bay, found there a ship and four sloops. Teach hoisted his

---

[1] **man-of-war** – a ship of the royal navy

[2] **slipped her cable** – left quickly by leaving the cable without taking time to weigh the anchor

flag and began to fire at them, at which the captain and his men left their ship and fled to the shore. Teach burned two of these sloops, and let the other three depart.

In the commonwealth of pirates, he who goes to the greatest length of wickedness is looked upon with a kind of envy among them, as a person of extraordinary bravery, and is thereby entitled to be distinguished by some post. And if such a one has but courage, he must certainly be a great man. The pirate of whom we are writing was thoroughly accomplished this way, and some of his wild amusements and wickedness were so extravagant that it seems as though he were trying to make his men believe he was a devil incarnate.

One day, being at sea and a little drunk, Blackbeard says, "Come, let us make a hell of our own and see how long we can bear it!" Accordingly he, with two or three others, went down into the hold. And, closing up all the hatches, they filled several pots full of brimstone and other burnable matter, and set it on fire.
This they continued till they were almost suffocated, when some of the men cried out for air. At last Blackbeard opened the hatches, not a little pleased that he had held out the longest.

One night, drinking in the cabin with Israel Hands, the pilot, and another man, Blackbeard, without any reason at all, secretly draws out a small pair of pistols, and cocks them under the table. This action was perceived by one of the men, who wisely left the cabin and went up on deck, leaving Hands, the pilot, and the captain together.

When the pistols were ready, Blackbeard blew out the candle and, crossing his hands, fired the pistols at his company. Hands the master was shot through the knee and crippled for life. The other pistol missed its aim.

Being asked the meaning of this, Blackbeard only answered, "If I do not now and then kill one of you, you shall forget who I am!"

They afterward sailed to different places, and having taken two small vessels, they anchored off the Bar of Charleston for a few days. Here they captured a ship bound for England as she was coming out of the harbor. They next seized a vessel coming out of Charleston, and two pinks[3] coming into the same harbor, together with a brigantine[4] with fourteen black men.

The audacity of these actions, performed in sight of the town, struck the inhabitants with terror, as they had been lately visited by some other notorious

---

[3] **pinks** – small, fast sailing vessels

[4] **brigantine** – a square-rigged ship with two masts

"LET US MAKE A HELL OF OUR OWN!"

pirates. Meanwhile there were eight ships in the harbor, none of which dare set to sea for fear of falling into the hands of Blackbeard. The trade of this place was totally interrupted, and the inhabitants were abandoned to despair. Their calamity was greatly increased from the fact that a long and desperate war with the natives had just ended when they began to be infested by these robbers.

    Teach and his pirates were soon in great need of medicines. He had kept as prisoners all the persons taken in the ships they had captured, and he had the audacity to demand a chest of medicines from the governor of the colony. This demand was made in a manner not less daring than insolent. Teach sent Richards (the captain of the *Revenge*) with Mr. Marks, one of the prisoners, and several others, to present their request. Richards informed the governor that unless their demand was granted and he and his companions returned in safety, every prisoner on board the captured ships would instantly be put to death, and the vessels would be burnt to ashes.

"IF I DON'T KILL ONE OF YOU, YOU'LL FORGET WHO I AM!"

During the time that Mr. Marks was negotiating with the governor, Richards and his associates walked the streets at pleasure, while indignation flamed from every eye against them, as the robbers of their property and the terror of their country.

Though the shameful defiance thus offered the Government was great and most boldly wicked, yet, to preserve the lives of so many men, the governor granted the pirate's request, and sent on board a chest of medicines valued at three or four hundred pounds.

COLONISTS FIGHTING THE SAVAGES

Teach, as soon as he received the medicines and his fellow pirates, pillaged the ships of gold and provisions, and then dismissed the prisoners with their vessels. From the Bar of Charleston they sailed to North Carolina.

Teach now began to consider how he could best secure the spoil, along with some of the crew who were his favorites. Accordingly, under the false appearance of cleaning,[5] he ran his vessel on shore and grounded. Then he ordered the men in Israel Hands' sloop to come to his assistance. When they tried to do this, they also ran aground, and so both ships were lost. Then Teach went into the tender[6] with forty hands and, upon a sandy island—about a league[7] from shore, where there was neither bird nor beast, nor herb for them to live upon—he marooned seventeen of his crew, who would certainly have perished had not Major Bonnet received word of their miserable situation and sent a longboat to rescue them.

After this barbarous deed, Teach, with the remainder of his crew, went to

---

[5] **cleaning** – burning off the seaweed and barnacles from a ship's bottom

[6] **tender** – small vessel employed to attend upon a larger one

[7] **league** – three nautical miles

the Governor of North Carolina and claimed the pardon offered by the king to all repentant pirates. He kept for himself and his crew all the treasures which had been acquired by his fleet.

This temporary interruption of the piratical plundering and violence of Blackbeard (for so he was now called), did not proceed from the conviction of his former errors, or a determination to reform, but only to prepare for future and more extensive exploits.

> *"It is as sport to a fool to do mischief."*
>
> — *Proverbs 10:23*

Chapter Six

Save the Ship!

To save the ship, rich cargo's cast away.
Your soul is shipwrecked if your lusts do stay.

In storms and distresses at sea, the richest merchandise is cast overboard. The sailors care not for them when life and all is in jeopardy and hazard (Jonah 1:5). The sailors cast forth the cargo that was in the ship into the sea to lighten it and, in Acts 27:18-19, they cast out the very tackling of the ship.

No matter how highly men prize such merchandise, yet reason tells them that it were better that these should perish rather than life be lost. Satan himself could say, "Skin for skin, and all that a man hath, he will give for his life" (Job 2:4).

Application

And surely it is every way as highly reasonable that men should mortify,[1] cast out, and cut off their dearest lusts, rather than their immortal souls should sink and perish in the storm of God's wrath. Life, indeed, is a precious treasure, and highly valued by men. You know what Solomon says: "a living dog is better than a dead lion" (Ecclesiastes 9:4).

---

[1] **mortify** – subdue (lusts) or bring them into subjection to the Law of God

And we find men willing to part with their estates, limbs, or any outward comfort for the preservation of their life. The woman in the gospel spent all she had on the physicians for her *health,* which is a degree below life. Some men indeed do much overvalue their lives, and part with Christ and peace of conscience for it. But he that thus saves his life shall lose it (Luke 9:24).

Now, if life be worth so much, what then is the soul worth? Alas! Life is but "a vapor, which appeareth for a little while, and then vanisheth away" (James 4:14). Life is indeed worth more than all the world, but my soul is worth more than ten thousand lives! Nature teaches you to value the first so high, and grace should teach you to value the second much higher (Matthew 6:25-33).

Now here is the case: either you must part with your sins or with your souls. If your sins be not cast out, both sin and soul must sink together. "If ye live after the flesh, ye must die" (Romans 8:13). God speaks to you as He did to Ahab when he spared Benhadad, "Because you have let go a sin, which God has appointed to destruction, therefore your life shall go for his life" (See 1 Kings 20:40). Guilt will raise a storm of wrath, as Jonah did, if not cast out.

Reflection

And must sin or the soul perish? Must my life, yes, my eternal life, pay for it if I spare sin? O then let me not be cruel to my own soul by sparing my sin! O my soul, this foolish pity and cruel indulgence will be your ruin! If I spare it, God has said that "He will not spare me" (Deuteronomy 29:20).

It is true, the pains of mortification[2] are sharp, but yet they are easier than the pains of hell. To cut off a right hand or pluck out a right eye, is hard; but to have my soul cut off eternally from God, is harder still. Is it as easy, O my soul, to burn from them in hell, as to mortify them on earth? Surely, it is "profitable for me, that one member perish, rather than all be cast into hell" (Matthew 5:29-30).

I see the merchant willing to part with rich goods and merchandise if his ship is caught in a storm. And those that have legs or arms afflicted with gangrene willingly stretch them out to be cut off in order to save their life. And shall I be willing to endure no difficulties for my soul? Christ looked upon souls as worth His blood, and is mine not worth my self-denial? Lord, let me not warm a snake in my bosom, that will at the end sting me to the heart!

> Your soul's the ship; its cargo is its lusts,
> God's judgments: stormy winds and dangerous gusts.
> Conscience the master; but the stubborn will
> Is master of the goods, and keeps the bill:
>
> Desires are all the men. The winds do rise,
> The storm increases; conscience gives advice
> To throw those lusts o'erboard, and so to ease
> The ship, or else it cannot keep the seas.

---

[2] **mortification** – the act of subduing (lusts) or bringing them into subjection to the Law of God

The will opposes, and the desires say
The master's counsel they will not obey.
The case is dangerous; that none can doubt,
Who sees the storm within, and that without.

Lusts and desires do not care for the weather.
They are resolved to swim or sink together.
Conscience still strives, but they cannot abide
That it, or reason, should the case decide.

Lust knows that reason in like cases still
Determines well. Then choose ye whom ye will.
Shall you hear Satan's words? His case has been
Before him, and he judged that, skin for skin,
And all men have, they'll part with for their life.
Then how unreasonable is this strife?

All those who do set sail with sins aboard,
And who within their lives do foul lusts hoard,
The storms shall trouble them within their ship,
And for their souls prepare a dreadful whip.

Chapter Seven

A Battle to the Death

"The righteousness of the perfect shall direct his way: but the wicked shall fall by his own wickedness."

— Proverbs 11:5

Before Teach entered upon his new adventures, he married a young woman of about sixteen years of age, the governor himself performing the ceremony. It was reported that this was only his fourteenth wife, about twelve of whom were yet alive. And, though this woman was young and lovely, he behaved towards her in a manner so brutal that was shocking to all decency and propriety, even among the unspeakably wicked race of pirates.

In his first voyage of piracy after he had obtained the king's pardon, Blackbeard directed his course to the Bermudas and, meeting with two or three English vessels, emptied them of

PORTRAIT OF BLACKBEARD THE PIRATE

their stores and other necessaries, and allowed them to proceed. He also met with two French vessels bound for Martinique, the one light, and the other loaded with sugar and cocoa. He put the men from the one into the other, and allowed her to depart. He then brought the loaded vessel into North Carolina, where the governor and Blackbeard shared the prizes.

Nor did their audacity and villainy stop here. Teach and some of his abandoned crew went to his Excellency the governor and swore that they had found the French ship at sea, without a soul on board. Therefore a court was called and the ship was condemned. The honorable governor received sixty hogsheads[1] of sugar for his share, his secretary twenty, and the pirates the remainder. But, as guilt always inspires suspicion, Teach was afraid that someone might arrive in the harbor that might detect the roguery. Therefore, upon the false declaration that the French ship was leaky, might sink, and so stop up the entrance to the harbor where she lay, they obtained the governor's liberty to drag her into the river, where she was set on fire, and when burnt down to the water, her bottom was sunk, so that she might never rise in judgment against them.

Blackbeard now being in the province of friendship, he passed several months in the river, giving and receiving visits from the planters, while he traded with the vessels which came to that river. Sometimes he traded in the way of lawful commerce, and sometimes in his own way. When he chose to appear the honest man, he made fair purchases on equal barter. But when this did not suit his needs or his present state of mind, he would rob at pleasure.

But there are limits to human insolence and depravity. The captains of the vessels who frequented that river, and had been so often harassed and plundered by Blackbeard, secretly consulted with some of the planters on what measures to pursue in order to banish such a detestable, vile wretch from their coasts, and to bring him to deserved punishment. Convinced from long experience that the governor himself, to whom it belonged, would give no assistance, they

Pirates feasting ashore

---

[1] **hogsheads** – large barrels

brought the matter to Alexander Spotswood, the governor of Virginia, and begged that an armed force might be sent from the men-of-war[2] lying there, either to take or to destroy those pirates who infested their coast.

At this request the governor of Virginia consulted with the captains of the two men-of-war as to the best measures to be adopted. It was resolved that the governor should hire two small vessels which could pursue Blackbeard into all his inlets and creeks; that they should be manned from the men-of-war, and the command given to Lieutenant Maynard, an experienced, bold, and determined

---

[2] **men-of-war** – ships of the royal navy

ALEXANDER SPOTSWOOD, GOVERNOR OF VIRGINIA

A Battle to the Death

officer.

When all was ready for his departure, the governor called an assembly, in which it was resolved to issue a proclamation offering a great reward to any who, within a year, should take or destroy any pirate.

Upon the 17th of November, 1717, Maynard left the James River in search of Blackbeard. This expedition was fitted out with all possible speed and secrecy, no boat being permitted to pass down the river that might convey any intelligence, while care was taken to discover where the pirates were lurking. And, on the evening of the 21st, he came in sight of the pirate.

Despite the secrecy and speed of the expedition, Blackbeard had already received some news of Maynard's coming. But the hardened, foolish pirate, having been often confused with false information, paid little heed to this information. Nor was he convinced of its accuracy until he saw the sloops sent to arrest him. Though Blackbeard had then only twenty men on board, he prepared to give battle.

Lieutenant Maynard arrived with his sloops in the evening, and anchored, as he could not venture under cloud of night to go into the place where Blackbeard lay. The pirate spent the night in drinking with the master of a trading vessel, with the same indifference as if no danger had been near. Nay, such was the desperate wickedness of this villain that it is reported that, during the noisy drinking party of that night, one of his men asked him:

"In case anything happens to you during the engagement with the two sloops that are waiting to attack you in the morning, does your wife know where you have buried your treasure?"

To this question Blackbeard impiously replied:

"Nobody but myself and the devil know where it is, and he who lives the longest shall take all."

In the morning Maynard weighed anchor and sent his boat to sound,[3] which, coming near, the pirate received her fire. Maynard then hoisted royal colors[4] and made directly towards Blackbeard with every sail and oar. In a little time the pirate ran aground, and so also did the king's vessels.

Maynard lightened his vessel by throwing overboard his ballast and barrels of water, and made towards Blackbeard. Upon

---

[3] **sound** – measure the depth of water

[4] **royal colors** – England's flag

this, Blackbeard hailed him in his own rude style:

"Curse you, ye villains! Who are you, and from where do you come?"

The Lieutenant answered, "You can see from our flags we are no pirates."

Blackbeard ordered Maynard to send his boat on board the pirate's ship, that Blackbeard might see who he was.

But Maynard replied, "I cannot spare my boat, but I will come on board of you as soon as I can with my sloop."

Upon this Blackbeard took a glass of liquor and drank to him, saying, "I'll give no quarters,[5] nor take any from you!"

Maynard replied, "I expect no quarters from you, nor shall I give you any." During this conversation the pirate's ship floated, and the sloops were rowing with all speed towards him. As she came near, the pirate fired a broadside charged with all manner of small shot, which killed or wounded twenty of Maynard's men. Blackbeard's ship soon after fell broadside to the shore. One of the sloops called the *Ranger* also fell astern.

But Maynard, finding that his own sloop had way and would soon be on board of Teach, ordered all his men down, while he himself and the man at the helm (whom he commanded to lie hidden), were the only persons who remained on deck. He at the same time commanded his men to take their pistols, cutlasses, and swords, and be ready for action upon his call. And, for greater speed, two ladders were placed in the hatchway.

When the King's sloop came alongside Blackbeard's vessel, the pirate's case-boxes[6] filled with powder, small-shot, slugs, and pieces of lead and iron, with a quick match in the mouth of them, were thrown into Maynard's sloop. Fortunately, however, the men were in the hold, and thus they did little injury on the present occasion, though they are usually very destructive.

---

[5] **quarters** – to spare the life of a captive or enemy

[6] **case-boxes** – an old form of shrapnel

"CUT TO PIECES THOSE THAT ARE STILL ALIVE!"

Blackbeard, seeing few or no men upon the deck of Maynard's ship, cried to his men: "They are all knocked on the head, except three or four! Now, therefore," says he, "let's jump on board, and cut to pieces those that are alive!"

Upon this, during the smoke caused by one of these case-boxes, Blackbeard, with fourteen of his men, boarded Maynard's ship, and were not perceived until the smoke cleared. Then the signal was given to Maynard's men, who rushed up in an instant. Blackbeard and the Lieutenant exchanged shots, and the pirate was wounded. Then they engaged sword in hand, until Maynard's sword broke. But fortunately one of his men at that instant gave Blackbeard a terrible wound in the neck and throat. The most desperate and bloody conflict followed, Maynard with twelve men and Blackbeard with fourteen. The sea was dyed with blood all around the vessel, and uncommon bravery was displayed upon both sides.

Though the pirate Blackbeard was wounded by the first shot from Maynard, yet he fought with desperate valor, though he had received twenty cuts and five more shot. Finally, when cocking his pistol, he fell down dead. By this time eight of his men had fallen, and the rest, being wounded, cried out for quarter, which was granted.

The other sloop also attacked the men who remained in the pirate vessels until they also cried out for quarter. And such was the desperation of Blackbeard that, having only a small hope of escaping, he had placed a black man with a match at the gunpowder-door, commanding him to blow up the ship the moment it was boarded by the King's men, in order to murder them all. That destructive broadside at the commencement of the action, however (which at first appeared so unlucky), was the means protecting them from the intended destruction.

Maynard severed the pirate's head from his body, suspended it upon his bowsprit-end, and sailed to Bath-town to obtain medical aid for his wounded men.

After his men were healed at Bath-town, the Lieutenant proceeded to Virginia, with the head of Blackbeard still suspended on his bowsprit-end, as a trophy of his victory, to the great joy of all the inhabitants. The prisoners were tried, condemned, and executed. And thus the crew of that infernal villain Blackbeard was destroyed.

> *"The righteousness of the perfect shall direct his way:*
> *but the wicked shall fall by his own wickedness."*
>
> *— Proverbs 11:5*

Chapter Eight

Your Gold or Your Life?

Men run such dangers, all for earthly gains,
But, for their souls, they'd ne'er take half the pains!

How exceedingly anxious and desirous are seamen for a small portion of the world! And how daring and bold are they in obtaining it! How extravagantly do they spend strength and life for it? They will run to the ends of the earth and engage in a thousand dangers, all upon the hopes and probability of getting a small possession of property or goods. Hopes of gain make them willing to risk their liberty—yea, their life—and encourages them to endure heat, cold, and hunger, and a thousand troubles and difficulties to which they are frequently exposed.

Application

How hot and eager are men's desires after the world! And how lazy and cold are they toward things eternal! They are worried and troubled about many things, but seldom pay heed to the great and necessary matters (Luke 10:40-42). They can rise early, go to bed late, and eat the bread of worry and care, but when did they so deny themselves for their poor souls? Their heads are full of plans and projects to get or advance their possessions. "We will go into such a city, and continue there a year, and buy and sell, and get gain" (James 4:13). This is the master-plan which engages all their time, studies, and plans. The will has passed a decree for it, the heart and desires are fully given over to it; they will be rich (1 Timothy 6:9).

The Spirit of God takes deep notice of this decree of the will. And, indeed, it is the clearest and fullest display of a man's heart and his condition. For look what is highest in a man's eyes, first and last in the thoughts, and upon which we spend our time and strength with delight—certainly, that is our treasure (Matthew 6:20-21). The heads and hearts of saints are full of anxious cares and fears about their spiritual condition. The great end and purpose they drive toward (to which all other things are but things in passing), is to make their calling and election sure. This is the weight and bias of their spirit. If their hearts stray and wander after any other things, this brings them back again.

Reflection

Lord, this has been my manner from my youth (may the carnal-minded man say). I have been laboring for the meat that perishes, worrying myself in vain, full of plans and projects for this world, and unwearied in my attempts to obtain an earthly treasure. Yet in this I have either been hindered and disappointed by providence; or, if I have obtained it, yet I no sooner begin to enjoy the pleasure and comfort I promised myself in it, when I am ready to leave it all, to be stripped out of it by death. And in that day all my thoughts perish.

But, in the meantime, what have I done for my soul? When did I ever lose a night's sleep, or deny and refuse myself for it? Ah, fool that I am! to nourish and pamper a vile body, which must shortly lie under the dust, and become a loathsome carcass! And, in the meantime, I have neglected and undone my poor soul, which shares in a nature like that of the angels, and must live for ever. I have kept other's vineyards, but mine own vineyard I have not kept (Song of Solomon 1:6). I have been an eternal laborer and slave to the world. My soul has been in a worse condition than the bodies of those condemned to work at the mines. Lord, change my treasure, and change my heart! O let it suffice, that I have been thus long laboring in the fire for nothing but vanity. Now gather up my heart and desires in Yourself, and let my great purpose now be to secure a special interest in Your blessed self, that I may once say, "To me to live is Christ!" (Philippians 1:21.)

>
> The face of man, impressed and stamped on gold,
> With crown, and royal scepters, we behold.
> No wonder that a human face gold gains,
> Since head, heart, soul, and body it obtains.
>
> Gold reigns as lord, and so it should behave,
> For all the world seeks to become its slave.
> Charmed with its clinking sound, away they go,
> Like vultures to the carcass, row upon row,
>
> Through worlds of dangers foolish creatures run,
> That into its embraces they may come.
> Poor slaves within the mines, my heart condoles,
> But seldom turns aside to pity souls,
>
> Which are the slaves indeed, that toil and spend
> Themselves upon gold's service. Surely, friend,
> They are but officers to dig and make
> Your grave within those mines, whence they do take
> And dig their ore. Ah! Many souls, I fear,
> Whose bodies live, yet lie entombed in here.
>
> Is gold so tempting to you? Lo, Christ stands,
> With length of days, and riches in His hands.
> Gold tried within the fire He freely gives,
> But few regard, or take that gold and live.

BARTHOLOMEW ROBERTS

The Dreaded Pirate Roberts

Chapter Nine

A Merry Life for Me!

"For the grace of God that bringeth salvation hath appeared to all men, teaching us that, denying ungodliness and worldly lusts, we should live soberly, righteously, and godly, in this present world."

— Titus 2:11-12

Bartholomew Roberts sailed as an honest man from London aboard the *Princess*, whose commander was Captain Plumb. Roberts was second mate of the ship. He left England November, 1719, and arrived at Guinea about February of the next year.

And, being at Anamaboe, he was taken captive by the pirate Captain Howel Davis. In the beginning Roberts was very opposed to the piratical sort of life, and would certainly have escaped from them had a fair opportunity presented itself. But afterwards he changed his mind, as many others besides him have done (and perhaps for the same reason too: preferment).[1] What he did not like as a member of the crew he could reconcile to his conscience when he became a commander.

After a time Captain Davis sailed to the Island of Princes, captured a French

---

[1] **preferment** – advancement to a higher office or station

ship, and was afterward killed by the Portuguese while attempting to raid the Island. The company of pirates therefore found themselves under the necessity of filling up Davis' post, for which there appeared two or three candidates among the leaders of the pirates, who styled themselves *lords*.

After discussing this matter, and how shattered and weak a condition their government must be without a head, my Lord Dennis (one of the pirates) proposed, it is said, over a bowl of rum, to this purpose:

"It is of no great significance who is dignified with the title of Captain, for really and in good truth all good governments have, like ours, the supreme power lodged with the community, who may doubtless appoint and revoke the man as suits their interest or humor. We are the original of this claim," says he, "and if a captain be so impudent as to go beyond his bounds at any time, why, down with him! His death will make his successors cautious of the fatal consequences that any sort of wrongful seizing of power might bring. However, it is my advice that while we are sober we decide upon a man of courage, and one who is skilled in navigation, someone who by his council and bravery seems best able to defend this commonwealth and protect us from the dangers and tempests of an unstable leader and the fatal consequences of anarchy. And such a one I take Roberts to be—a fellow, I think, in all respects worthy of your esteem and favor."

This speech was loudly applauded by all except Lord Sympson, who had secret hopes himself of being Captain. But, at this disappointment, he grew sullen and left them, swearing, "I do not care who you choose as captain."

Roberts was accordingly elected, though he had not been among the pirates more than six weeks. The choice was confirmed by all, and he accepted the honor, saying:

"Since I have dipped my hands in muddy water and must

be a pirate, it is better to be a commander than a common man."

Roberts was a tall dark man, near forty years of age, of good abilities and personal bravery, though he applied them to such wicked purposes as to make them completely despicable and unpraiseworthy. When drinking he frequently toasted "Curses to him who ever lives to wear a halter."[2] He was at first forced into piracy himself when his ship was taken by pirates. At that time he shed many crocodile tears at his fate. But, as he would tell the new men, time and good company had worn it off. He could not claim that he lacked means of employment or ability to get his bread in an honest way, to favor so vile a change. Nor was he so much a coward as to pretend it, but frankly confessed it was to get rid of the disagreeable superiority of some masters he was acquainted with, and the love of novelty and change that ocean wanderings had accustomed him to.

"In an honest service," says he, "there is little food, low wages, and hard work. In the pirate service, there is plenty and to spare, pleasure and ease, freedom and power. Who then would not choose the pirate life, even with all its dangers, when the worst that can happen is a chance or two at hanging? No, 'a merry life and a short one' shall be my motto."

---

[2] **wear a halter** – be hanged

Thus he preached himself into an approval of what he at first abhorred, and being daily entertained with music, drinking, and the merriment and amusements of his companions, these depraved inclinations were quickly edged and strengthened, and soon extinguished fear and conscience.

As soon as the government was settled by promoting other officers in the place of those who were killed with Captain Davis, the company resolved to avenge Captain Davis' death, he being more than ordinarily respected by the crew for his good nature as well as his conduct and bravery upon all occasions.

Therefore about thirty men were landed in order to make an attack upon the fort, which must be ascended to by a steep hill facing the mouth of the cannon. These men were headed by one Kennedy, a bold, daring fellow, but very wicked and vicious. They marched directly up under the fire of their ship guns, and as soon as they were discovered, the Portuguese left their post and fled to the town, and the pirates marched in without opposition, set fire to the fort, and threw all the guns off the hill into the sea. After they had done this, they retreated quietly to their ship.

But the pirates did not look upon this as a sufficient satisfaction for the injury they had received. Therefore most of the company desired to burn the town. Roberts said he would yield to their wishes if any plan could be proposed of doing it without their own destruction, for the town was more securely situated than the fort. A thick wood came almost close to it, giving cover to the defendants who, under such an advantage (he told them), it was to be feared would fire and stand better to their arms. Besides, bare houses would be but a slender reward for their trouble and loss.

This prudent advice prevailed. However, the pirates mounted the French ship they seized at this place with twelve guns, and sailed to the town and battered down several houses. After this they all returned on

board, gave back the French ship to her owners, and sailed out of the harbor by the light of two Portuguese ships, which they were pleased to set on fire there.

    Roberts sailed away to the southward, and met with a Dutch Guineaman, which he made prize of. But, after having plundered her, he gave the skipper back his ship again. Two days afterward he took an English ship called the *Experiment*. The men all entered into the pirate service and, having no use for the ship, they burnt her and then steered for St. Thomas.

But, meeting with nothing in their way, they sailed for Annabona, and there watered,[3] took in provisions, and put it to a vote of the company whether their next voyage should be to the East Indies or to Brazil. Brazil was decided upon, and they sailed accordingly, and in twenty-eight days arrived at Ferdinando, an uninhabited island on that coast. Here they took in water, cleaned their ship, and made ready for the intended cruise.

Upon this coast our rovers cruised for about nine weeks, keeping generally out of sight of land, but without seeing a sail, which discouraged them so much that they determined to leave the station and steer for the West Indies. And, in order to do this, they stood in toward land and fell in unexpectedly with a fleet of forty-two sail of Portuguese ships off the bay of Los Todos Santos, with all their cargo in, for Lisbon, several of them of good force, who were waiting for two men-of-war of seventy guns each, which would make up their convoy.

However, Roberts thought it should go hard with him, but he would make up his market among them, and therefore mixed with the fleet, keeping his men hidden till proper resolutions could be formed. That done, they came close up to one of the deepest ships, and ordered her to send the master on board quietly, threatening to give them no quarter if any resistance or signal of distress was made. The Portuguese, being surprised at these threats and the sudden flourish of cutlasses from the pirates, submitted without a word, and the captain came on board.

Roberts saluted him after a friendly manner, telling him that they were gentlemen of fortune, but that he only wanted to know which was the richest ship in that fleet. And if the master directed them rightly, he should be restored to his ship without molestation. If not, he must expect immediate death.

At this the Portuguese master pointed to a ship of forty guns and a hundred and fifty men, a ship of greater force than the *Rover*, but this in no way dismayed them; they were Portuguese, they said, and so immediately steered away for him. When they came within hail, the master whom they had a prisoner was ordered to ask "how Seignior Captain did?" and to invite him on board, "for that he had a matter of importance to discuss with him."

When this was done, the Captain responded that "he would wait upon him presently." But, by the bustle that immediately followed, the pirates perceived that they were discovered, and that this was only a deceitful answer of the captain's to

---

[3] **watered** – filled their casks with water

gain time to put his ship in a position of defense. So without further delay they poured in a broadside, boarded the ship, and grappled her. The dispute was short and warm, and many of the Portuguese fell, but two only of the pirates.

By this time the fleet was alarmed. Signals flew and guns were fired to alert the men-of-war, who rode still at anchor, and made but little haste out to their assistance. (And, if what the pirates themselves say is true, the commanders of those ships were blamable to the highest degree, and unworthy the title—or even the name—of men. For they were afraid to attack the pirate, and delayed so long that Roberts had time to leisurely make his way off.)

The pirates found this ship exceedingly rich, being loaded chiefly with sugar, skins, and tobacco, and in gold forty thousand *moidores* (a gold coin from Portugal), besides chains and trinkets of considerable value, particularly a cross set with diamonds designed for the king of Portugal.

Delighted with this booty, the pirates had nothing now to think of but some safe retreat where they might give themselves up to all the pleasures that luxury, loose living, and wickedness could bestow. For the moment they decided upon a place called the Devil's Islands in the river of Surinam on the coast of Guiana, where they arrived and found the best reception imaginable, not only from the governor and factory, but also from their wives, who exchanged wares and drove a considerable trade with the pirates.

The pirates seized in this river a sloop, and by her gained intelligence that a brigantine[4] had also sailed in company with her from Rhode Island, laden with provisions for the coast—a welcome cargo! The pirates were growing short in the sea store, and, as Sancho says, "No adventures are to be made without belly-timber."

One evening, as they were rummaging their mine of treasure, the Portuguese prize, this expected vessel was spied from the masthead, and Roberts, imagining nobody could do the business so well as himself, took forty men in the sloop and went in pursuit of her.

But a fatal accident followed this rash, though inconsiderable adventure, for Roberts, thinking of nothing less than bringing in the brigantine that afternoon, never troubled his head about the sloop's provisions, nor inquired what there was on board to feed such a number of men. But out he sails after his expected prize, which he not only lost further sight of, but after eight days' fighting with contrary winds and currents, they found themselves thirty leagues[5] out of their way. The current still opposing their endeavors, and perceiving no hopes of catching up to their ship, they came to an anchor, and inconsiderately sent away the boat to inform the rest of the company of their condition, and to order the ship to come to them.

But too soon—even the next day—their needs made them sensible of their foolhardiness, for their water was all gone, and they had taken no thought of how they would be supplied till either the ship came or the boat returned, which was not likely to be for another five or six days. At last they were driven to such extremity that they

---

[4] **brigantine** – a square-rigged ship with two masts

[5] **thirty leagues** – ninety nautical miles

were forced to tear up the floor of the cabin and patch up a sort of tub or raft with ropes to paddle ashore and fetch off immediate supplies of water to preserve their lives.

After some days the long-wished-for boat came back, but with the most unwelcome news in the world. For Kennedy (who was lieutenant, and who had been left to command the privateer and prize), had run off with both. This was humiliation with a vengeance, and you may imagine that they did not depart without some hard speeches from those that were left and had suffered by their treachery. And, that there need be no further mention of this Kennedy and his crew, I shall tell you now that they were soon captured, tried, and hung at Execution Dock.

Thus we see what a disastrous fate ever attends the wicked, and how rarely they escape the punishment due to their crimes, who, abandoned to such a vicious life, rob, spoil, and prey upon mankind contrary to the light and law of nature, as well as the Law of God. It might have been hoped that the examples of these deaths would have been as a lighthouse to the remainder of this gang, showing them how to shun the rocks their companions had wrecked upon.

It might have been hoped that the rest of the pirates would have surrendered to mercy, or divided themselves forever from such pursuits, for they might surely know that the same law and punishment awaited them, which they certainly agreed that they now equally deserved. Here was an impending law which never let them sleep well unless they were drunk. But all the use that was made of it here was to commend the justice of the court that condemned Kennedy, for he was a sad dog, they said, and deserved the fate he met with.

*"For the grace of God that bringeth salvation hath appeared to all men,
teaching us that, denying ungodliness and worldly lusts,
we should live soberly, righteously, and godly, in this present world."*

— Titus 2:11-12

Chapter Ten

The Deadliest Battle of All

How small a rudder turns a ship about?
Yet we, against our conscience, fight it out.

It is a thing worthy of admiration to see so great an object as a ship is—and when under sail, too, before a fresh and strong wind, by which it is carried as the clouds with marvelous force and speed—yet to be commanded with ease by so small a thing as a helm or rudder. The Scripture takes notice of it as a matter worthy of our consideration. "Behold also the ships, which though they be great, and driven of fierce winds, yet they are turned about with a small helm, whithersoever the governor listeth" (James 3:4).

Application

Just as a rudder in a ship, so has God designed the conscience in man to act for the whole man. This conscience, being steered and regulated by the Word and Spirit of God, is to steer and order man's whole life. Conscience is as the messenger of God, the judge and determiner of our actions, whether they be good or evil. And it lays the strongest obligations upon the creature to obey its commands, that is imaginable: For it binds under the reason and consideration of the most absolute and sovereign will of the great God.

So that, as often as conscience from the Word convinces us of any sin or duty, it lays such a bond upon us to obey it as no power under heaven can relax or do away with it. Angels cannot do it, much less man; for that would be to exalt themselves above God. Now, therefore, it is a high and dreadful way of sinning, to oppose and rebel against the conscience when it convinces of sin or duty. Conscience sometimes reasons it out with men, and shows them the necessity of changing their way and course, arguing it from the clearest and most accepted principles of right reason, as well as from the indisputable sovereignty of God.

As, for instance, it convinces our very minds that eternal matters are infinitely to be preferred over all momentary and perishing things (Romans 8:18; Hebrews 11:26). And it is our duty to choose them, and make all earthly and temporary matters to stand aside and give place to eternal things. Yet, though men be convinced of this, their stubborn will stands out, and will not yield up itself to the conviction of their conscience.

Further, conscience argues from this acknowledged truth that all the delights and pleasures of this world are but a miserable portion, and that it is the highest folly to risk an immortal soul for them (Luke 9:25). Alas! What remembrance is there of earthly pleasures in hell? They are as the waters that pass away. What will then be left of all their mirth and jollity but a tormenting sting!

Conscience convinces them clearly, also, that in deep matters of concernment it is a high point of wisdom to lay hold of and improve the right seasons and opportunities. "He that gathereth in summer is a wise son" (Proverbs 10:5). "A wise man's heart discerneth both time and judgment" (Ecclesiastes 8:5). There is a season to every purpose (Ecclesiastes 3:1), that is, a nick of time, a timely moment when, if a man strikes, he does his work effectively and with much ease. Such seasons conscience convinces the soul of, and often whispers thus in its ear:

"Now, soul, strike in, close with this moving of the Spirit, and be happy for ever. You may never have such a wind for heaven anymore."

Now, though these be accepted principles of reason, and though conscience enforce them strongly on the soul, yet it cannot prevail. The proud, stubborn will rebels, and will not be guided by it. (See Ephesians 2:3; Job 34:37; Isaiah 46:12; Ezekiel 2:4; Jeremiah 44:16.)

Reflection

Ah! Lord, such a heart have I had before You! How obstinate, how rebellious, and how uncontrollable by conscience it is! Many a time conscience has whispered thus in my ear, and many a time it has stood in my way, as the angel did in Balaam's, or the cherubims that kept the way of the tree of life with flaming swords turning every way (Numbers 22:22; Genesis 3:24). So has my conscience stood to oppose me in the way of my lusts.

How often has it calmly debated the case with me alone? And how sweetly

has it reasoned with me? How clearly has it convinced me of sin, danger, duty, with strong evidence? How terribly has it threatened my soul and set the point of the threatening at my very breast? And yet my head-strong desires will pay it no heed. I have obeyed the voice of every lust and temptation (Titus 3:3), but conscience has lost its authority with me. Ah, Lord! What a sad condition am I in, with regard both to sin and misery! My sin receives dreadful aggravations, for rebellion and presumption are thus added to it. I have violated the strongest bonds that were ever laid upon a creature.

If my conscience had not thus convinced and warned me, my sin would not have been so great and blood-red (James 4:17). Ah! This is to sin with a high hand, to sin presumptuously (Numbers 15:30), to come near to the great and unpardonable transgression (Psalm 19:13).

O how dreadful a way of sinning is this, with opened eyes! And, because my sin is thus immeasurably sinful, so my punishment will be immeasurably dreadful, if I continue in this rebellion. Lord, You have said, "Such shall be beaten with many stripes" (Luke 12:47). Yes, Lord, and if ever my conscience, which by rebellion is now grown silent, should be in judgment awakened in this life—O! what a hell should I have within me! How greatly would it thunder and roar upon me, and surround me with terrors!

Your word assures me that no length of time can wear out of its memory what I have done (Genesis 42:21). No violence or force can suppress it (Matthew 27:4). No greatness of power can stifle it; it will take the mightiest ruler by the throat (Exodus 10:16; Daniel 5:6). No music, pleasures, or delights can charm it (Job 20:22). O conscience! You are the sweetest friend or the dreadfulest enemy

in the world. Your comforts are unspeakably sweet, and your terrors cannot be endured. Ah! Let me stand it out no longer against conscience! The very ship in which I sail contradicts and refutes my madness, that rushes greedily into sin against both reason and conscience, and will not be commanded by it. Surely, O my soul, this will be bitterness in the end!

> A ship of greatest burden will obey
> The rudder; he that sits at helm may sway
> And guide its motion. If the pilot please,
> The ship bears up against both wind and seas.
>
> My soul's the ship, desires are its sails,
> Conscience the rudder. Ah, but Lord, what ails
> My wicked heart, to shuffle in and out
> When its convictions bid it turn about?
>
> Temptations blow a counter blast, and drive
> The vessel where they please, though conscience strive;
> And by its strong persuasions it will force
> My stubborn will to bear another course.
>
> Lord, if I run this course, Your Word does tell
> How quickly I shall soon arrive in hell.
> Then purify my conscience, change my will,
> Blow in Your pleasant winds, my God, and fill
>
> All my affections, and let nothing carry
> My soul from its due course, or make it vary.
> Then, if the pilot's work You will perform,
> I shall bear bravely up against a storm.

Chapter Eleven

Wine, Water, and Deserters

"A righteous man regardeth the life of his beast: but the tender mercies of the wicked are cruel."

— *Proverbs 12:10*

Let us now return to Roberts, whom we left on the coast of Guiana in a grievous passion at what Kennedy and the crew had done, and who was now projecting new adventures with his small company in the sloop. They here formed a set of articles to be signed and sworn to for the better preservation of their society. They excluded all Irishmen from their company, to whom they had a deep-seated hatred because of Kennedy, who was Irish.

Why Roberts could think that an oath would be binding upon men who had defied the laws of God and man, I cannot tell, but he thought their greatest security lay in this, that "It is in everyone's interest to observe these articles, if they desire to keep up so abominable a company."

And now, seeing the disadvantages they were now under, having a small, ill-repaired vessel and no provisions or stores, they resolved one and all to proceed for the West Indies, not doubting that they could there find a remedy for all these evils, and recover their loss.

In the latitude of Deseada (one of the islands) they took two sloops, which supplied them with provisions and other necessaries, and a few days afterwards took a brigantine belonging to Rhode Island.

They then proceeded to Barbados, off of which island they fell in with a Bristol ship of ten guns, from whom they took an abundance of clothes, some money, twenty-five bales of goods, five barrels of powder, a cable, ten casks of oatmeal, six casks of beef, and several other goods, besides five of their men. And after they had detained the ship three days they let her go—who, being bound for the island, she informed the governor of what had happened as soon as she arrived.

Because of this a Bristol galley that lay in the harbor was ordered to be fitted out with twenty guns and eighty men with all possible speed, there being then no man-of-war upon that station. They also ordered out a sloop with ten guns and forty men.

The galley was commanded by one Captain Rogers, of Bristol, and the sloop by Captain Graves, of that island. By a commission from the governor, Captain Rogers was appointed commodore.

The second day after Rogers sailed out of the harbor he was discovered by Roberts, who, knowing nothing of their intention, chased them. The Barbados ships kept an easy sail till the pirates came up with them, and then Roberts fired a cannon at them, expecting they would have immediately surrendered to his piratical flag. But instead he was forced to receive the fire of a broadside, with three huzzas at the same time, so that a battle ensued. But Roberts, barely holding his own, was obliged to crowd all the sail the sloop would bear to escape from the galley.

The galley, sailing pretty well, kept company for a long while, keeping up a constant fire which galled the pirate. However, finally, by throwing overboard their guns and other heavy goods and thereby lightening the vessel, they with much difficulty got away. But Roberts could never endure a Barbados man afterwards, and when any ships belonging to that island fell into his hands, he was more particularly brutal to them than to others.

Captain Roberts sailed in the sloop to the island of Dominico, where he took in water and got provisions from the inhabitants, to whom he gave goods in exchange. At this place he met with thirteen Englishmen who had been set ashore by a French sloop who had seized their ships as prizes. The men willingly entered in with the pirates, and it proved a timely recruit.

They stayed not long here, though they had immediate occasion for cleaning¹ their sloop, but did not think this a proper place. Therefore they made

---
¹ **cleaning** – burning off the seaweed and barnacles from a ship's bottom

haste from the island, for, as they themselves had the impudence to declare, there was a terrible scarcity of wine and women.

Thus they sailed for Newfoundland, and arrived upon the banks the end of June, 1720. They entered the harbor of Trepassi with their black colors flying, drums beating, and trumpets sounding. There were twenty-two vessels in the harbor, from which the men all fled upon the sight of the pirate, and hastened ashore.

It is impossible particularly to recount the destruction and havoc they made here, burning and sinking all the shipping except a Bristol galley, and destroying the fisheries of the poor planters without any remorse or twinge of conscience.

Indeed, nothing is so lamentable and grievous as power in wicked and ignorant hands. It makes men immoral and unrestrained, unstable and wild, unconcerned at the misfortunes they are imposing on their fellow-creatures. It keeps them smiling at the mischiefs that bring themselves no advantage or benefit. They are like madmen that cast firebrands, arrows, and death, and say, "Are not we in sport?"[2] (Proverbs 26:18-19.)

Roberts manned the Bristol galley he took in the harbor and mounted sixteen guns on board her. And, cruising out upon the banks, he met with nine or ten sail of French ships, all of which he destroyed except one of twenty-six guns, which they seized and carried off for their own use. This ship they christened the *Fortune* and, leaving the Bristol galley to

the Frenchmen, they sailed away in company with the sloop on another cruise, and took several prizes: the *Richard* of Biddeford, the *Willing Mind* of Pool, the *Expectation* of Topsham, and the *Samuel* of London. Out of these ships they increased their company by entering all the men they could well spare in their own service.

The *Samuel* was a rich ship and had several passengers on board, who were treated very roughly in order to make them reveal the location of their money. The pirates threatened them every moment with death if they did not deliver everything up to them. They tore up the hatches and entered the hold like a parcel of demons, and with axes and cutlasses cut and broke open all the bales, cases, and boxes they could lay their hands on. And when any goods came upon deck that they did not like to carry aboard, instead of tossing them into the hold again, they threw them overboard into the sea. All this was done with incessant cursing and swearing, more like demons than men. They carried away with them sails, guns, powder, cordage, and £8,000 or £9,000 worth of the choicest goods, and told Captain Cary of the *Samuel*:

"We will not go to Hope Point to be hanged up a-sun-drying, as Kidd's and Braddish's company were. But if we are ever overpowered, we'll set fire to the powder with a pistol, and go all merrily to hell together."

After they had brought all the booty aboard, a consultation was held whether

they should sink or burn the ship. But, while they were debating the matter, they spied a sail, and so left the *Samuel* to give her chase.

At midnight they came up with the ship, which proved to be a snow[3] from Bristol, bound for Boston, with Captain Bowles as master. They treated him barbarously because Captain Rogers, his countryman (who attacked them off Barbados), was of the city of Bristol.

July 16th, which was two days afterwards, they took a Virginia ship called the *Little York*, and the *Love* of Liverpool, which they plundered and let go. The next day a snow from Bristol, called the *Phoenix*, met with the same fate from them, as also a brigantine and a sloop called the *Sadbury*. They took all the men out of the brigantine and sunk the vessel.

In this ship Roberts then proceeded for the coast of Guinea, but before they reached it he proposed to touch at Brava, the southernmost of the Cape Verde Islands, and clean. But here again, by an intolerable stupidity and lack of judgment, they got so far to leeward[4] of their port that, despairing of regaining it, they were obliged to go back again for the West Indies, which very nearly was the destruction of them all.

Surinam was the place now designed for, which was at no less than 700 leagues[5] distance, and they had but one hogshead[6] of water left to supply 124 souls for that passage—a sad circumstance that abundantly reveals the folly and madness among pirates. And he must be an inconsiderate wretch indeed who, if he could separate the wickedness and punishment from the fact, would yet risk his life amid such dangers as their lack of skill and foresight made them liable to.

---

[3] **snow** – a two-masted vessel

[4] **leeward** – opposite side from which the wind is blowing

[5] **league** – three nautical miles

[6] **hogshead** – large barrel

Their sins, we may presume, were never so troublesome to their memories as now that inevitable destruction seemed to threaten them, without the least glimpse of comfort or alleviation to their misery. For with what face could wretches who had ravaged and made so many poor and needy, look up for relief? They had to that moment lived in defiance of the Power that now alone they must trust for their preservation, and indeed without the miraculous intervention of Providence there appeared only this miserable choice, either a present death by their own hands, or a lingering one by starvation.

They continued their course, and came to an allowance of one single mouthful of water for twenty-four hours. Many of them drank sea-water which, instead of quenching, gave them an inextinguishable thirst that killed them. Others pined and wasted away with disease, so that they dropped away daily. Those that sustained the misery best were such as almost starved themselves, forbearing all sorts of food, unless a mouthful or two of bread the whole day, so that those who survived were as weak as was possible for men to be and still be alive.

But if the dismal prospect they set out with gave them anxiety, trouble, or pain, what must their fears and terrors be when they had not one drop of water left, or any other liquid to moisten or revive? This was their case when (by the working of Divine Providence, no doubt) at night they anchored in seven fathoms of water. This was an inexpressible joy to them and, as it were, fed the expiring lamp of life with fresh spirits. But this could not hold long. When the morning came they saw land from the mast-head, but it was at so great a distance that it offered but a faint hope to men who had drunk nothing for the last two days. However, they sent their boat away, and late the same night it returned—to their no small comfort—with a load of water, informing them that they had got off the mouth of Meriwinga River on the coast of Surinam.

One would have thought that so miraculous an escape would have worked some reformation among them, but, alas! they had no sooner quenched their thirst than they forgot the miracle, till scarcity of provisions awakened their senses and bid them guard against starving. Their allowance was very small, and yet they would profanely say, "The Providence which gave us drink will, no doubt, bring us meat also, if we use but an honest endeavor."

In pursuance of these "honest endeavors," they were steering for the latitude of Barbados, with what little they had left, to look out for more or starve. And in their way they met a ship that answered their necessities, and after that a brigantine.

Out of the ship and brigantine the pirates got a good supply of provisions and liquor, so that they gave up the intended cruise. And, hearing of two sloops that had been fitted and sent after them at Corvocoo, they sailed to the island of Martinique to make the governor some sort of a present, in response to the care and speed he had shown in sending out warships after them.

It is the custom at Martinique for the Dutch smugglers that desire to trade with the people of the island to hoist their flags when they come before the town. Roberts knew the signal and, being an utter enemy to them, he bent his thoughts on mischief, and accordingly came in with his flag flying, which, as he expected, they mistook for a good market, and thought themselves happiest that could soonest

send off their sloops and vessels for trade.

When Roberts had got them within his power, one after another, he told them he would not have it said that they came off for nothing, and therefore ordered them to leave their money behind, for that they were a parcel of rogues, and he hoped they would always meet with such a Dutch trade as this was. He reserved one vessel to set the passengers on shore again, and set fire to the rest, to the number of twenty.

Roberts was so enraged at the attempts that had been made by the governors of Barbados and Martinique for capturing him that he ordered a new flag to be made, which they ever after hoisted, with his own figure portrayed standing upon two skulls. And under the skulls were the letters A. B. H. and A. M. H., signifying a Barbadian's and a Martinican's head.

At Dominico (the next island they stopped at), they took a Dutch smuggler of twenty-two guns and seventy-five men, and a brigantine belonging to Rhode Island. The smuggler made some defense until, by some of his men being killed, the rest were discouraged and surrendered.

With these two prizes they went down to Guadalupe, and brought out a sloop and a French fly-boat laden with sugar. The sloop they burnt, and went on to Moonay, another island, thinking to clean. But, finding the sea ran too high there to undertake it with safety, they bent their course for the north part of Hispaniola, where they cleaned both the ship and the brigantine.

While they were here two sloops came in (as they pretended), to pay Roberts a visit. The masters, whose names were Porter and Tuckerman, addressed the pirate as the Queen of Sheba did Solomon, to wit, "that having heard of his fame and achievements," they had put in there to learn his skill and wisdom in the business of pirating, being vessels on the same honorable design with himself. They hoped that, with the sharing of his knowledge, they would also receive his charity, being in want of necessaries for such adventures. Roberts was

"Curse ye all, gentlemen!"

won upon by the peculiarity and bluntness of these two men, and gave them powder, arms, and whatever else they had occasion for, spent two or three merry nights with them, and at parting, said, "I do hope the Lord will prosper your handiworks."

They passed some time here, after they had got their vessel ready, in their usual loose and wicked living. They had taken a considerable quantity of rum and sugar, so that liquor was as plentiful as water, and few there were who denied themselves the immoderate use of it. Nay, sobriety brought a man under a suspicion of being in a plot against the commonwealth, and in their sense he was looked upon to be a villain who would not be drunk.

This was evident in the affair of Harry Glasby, chosen master of the *Royal Fortune* who, with two others, laid hold of the opportunity at the last island they were at, to desert, and moved off without bidding farewell to his friends. Glasby was a reserved, sober man, and therefore gave occasion to be suspected, so that he was soon missed after he went away. And, a detachment being sent in search of the deserters, they were all three brought back again next day. This was a capital offense, and for which they were ordered to be brought to an immediate trial.

The place appointed for their trials was the steerage[7] of the ship, in order to which a large bowl of rum punch was made and placed upon the table and, the pipes and tobacco being ready, the judicial proceedings began.

The prisoners were brought forth, and articles of indictment against them read. They were charged with breaking a statute of their own making, and the letter of the law being strong against them and the fact plainly proved, they were about to pronounce sentence when one of the judges moved that they should first smoke the other pipe, which was accordingly done.

All the prisoners pleaded for mercy very movingly, but the court had such an abhorrence of their crime that they could not be prevailed upon to show mercy till one of the judges, whose name was Valentine Ashplant, stood up and, taking his pipe out of his mouth, said he had something to offer to the court in behalf of one of the prisoners, and spoke to this effect:

"Glasby shall not die; may I be cursed if he shall." After this scholarly speech he sat down in his place and resumed his pipe. This motion was loudly opposed by all the rest of the judges in similar terms, but Ashplant, who was resolute in his opinion, made another pathetical speech in the following manner:

"Curse ye all, gentlemen! I am as good a man as the best of you. May my soul be eternally damned if ever I turned my back to any man in my life, or ever will. Glasby is an honest fellow, despite this misfortune, and I love him. I hope he'll live and repent of what he has done, but if he must die, I will die along with him."

And thereupon he pulled out a pair of pistols and presented them to some of the learned judges upon the bench, who,

---

[7] **steerage** – area located below the quarterdeck

perceiving his argument so well supported, thought it reasonable that Glasby should be acquitted; and so they all came over to his opinion, and allowed it to be law.

But the only mercy that could be obtained for the other prisoners was that they should have the liberty of choosing any four of the whole company to be their executioners. The poor wretches were tied immediately to the mast and there shot dead, in accordance with their villainous sentence.

After this they put to sea again. With the *Royal Fortune* and the brigantine, which they christened the *Good Fortune,* they pushed towards the latitude of Deseada, to look out for provisions (being very short again), and, just to their wish, Captain Hingstone's ill fortune brought him in their way, richly laden for Jamaica. Him they carried to Bermuda and plundered.

And, sailing back again to the West Indies, they continually met with some consignment or other (chiefly French) which stored them with plenty of provisions and recruited their starving condition, so that, stocked with this sort of ammunition, they began to think of something worthier their aim. For these robberies that only supplied what was constantly used up by no means answered their intentions, and accordingly they proceeded again for the coast of Guinea, where they thought to buy gold dust very cheaply. In their passage there they took numbers of ships of all nations, some of which they burnt or sunk, as the actions or characters of the masters displeased them.

*"A righteous man regardeth the life of his beast:
but the tender mercies of the wicked are cruel."*

— *Proverbs 12:10*

Chapter Twelve

Sharks on Land

In seas, the greater fish the less devour.
So some men crush all those within their power.

There are fishes of prey in the sea as well as birds and beasts on the land. Our seamen tell us of the devouring whales, sharks, dolphins, and other fishes who follow the smaller fish and devour multitudes of them.

It is frequent with us in our own seas to find several smaller fishes in the bellies of the greater ones. Indeed, I have often heard seamen say that the poor little fry, when pursued, are so sensible of the danger, that they have sometimes seen multitudes of them throw themselves upon the shore and perish there, to avoid the danger of being devoured by the larger fish.

Application

So also are cruel, merciless, and oppressive wicked men, whose tender mercies are cruelty (Proverbs 12:10). We see the same cruelty in our evil creditors and over-reaching sharks ashore, who grind the faces of the poor, and regard not the cries of the fatherless and widows, but fill their houses with the gain of oppression. These are, by the Holy Spirit, compared to the fishes of the sea (Habakkuk 1:13-14).

This is a crying sin, yea, it sends up a loud cry to heaven for vengeance: "If thou afflict the widow and the fatherless, and they cry unto Me, I will surely hear their cry" (Exodus 22:23). "I will hear his cry, for I am gracious" (Exodus 22:27).

Nay, God will not only hear their cry, but will also avenge their quarrel. This is a remarkable text, "That no man go beyond and defraud his brother in any matter, because that the Lord is the avenger of all such" (1 Thessalonians 4:6). This word *avenger* is only used once more in the New Testament (in Romans 13:4). And there it is applied to the civil magistrate, who is to see execution done upon offenders.

But now this is a sin that sometimes may be out of the reach of man's justice, and therefore God Himself will be their avenger. You may overpower the poor in this world, and it may be they cannot contend with you at man's justice seat. Therefore God will bring it before His throne of judgment.

Believe it, sirs, this is a sin so provoking to God, that He will not let it escape without severe punishment sooner or later. The prophet Habakkuk wondered how the holy God could leave such wickedness alone till the general day of reckoning, and asked God why He did not take vengeance on them in this life as an example to other evil-doers. "Thou art of purer eyes than to behold evil, and canst not look upon iniquity. Wherefore then lookest Thou upon them that deal treacherously, and holdest Thy tongue when the wicked devours the man that is more righteous than he?" (Habakkuk 1:13.)

And see also Proverbs 23:10-11: "Enter not into the fields of the fatherless," that is, of the poor and helpless. But why is it more dangerous to violently invade their right than another's? The reason is added: "for their Redeemer is mighty, and He shall plead their cause with thee." It may be that they are not able to plead their cause. Here, therefore, God will plead their cause for them.

Reflection

Turn in upon yourself, O my soul, and consider: have you not been guilty of this crying sin? Have I not over-reached and defrauded[1] others, and filled my master's house with violence and deceit? And have I not thus brought myself under that dreadful curse of Zephaniah 1:9?

Or since I came to trade and deal upon mine own account, have not the scales of deceit been in my hand? I have (it may be) kept many in my service and employment. Have not I used their labors without reward, and so am under that woe of Jeremiah

---

[1] **defrauded** – wrongfully withheld something from another; deprived someone of their right

22:13? Or have I held back the wages they deserved for their work? (Isaiah 58:3.) Or, by bad payment and unjust deductions and allowances, have I defrauded them of a part of what is due them? (Malachi 3:5.) Or have I at least delayed payment out of a covetous desire to gain by it, while their necessities in the meantime cried aloud for it; and so have I sinned against God's express commands? (Deuteronomy 24:14-15; Leviticus 19:13.)

Or have I persecuted those whom God has smitten? (Psalm 69:26.) And have I rigorously exacted the utmost of my due, though the hand of God has gone out against them, breaking their estates? O my soul, examine yourself upon these particular matters. Rest not quiet until this guilt be removed by the application of the blood of sprinkling. Has not the Lord said that "they shall have judgment without mercy, that have shewed no mercy"? (James 2:13.) And is it not a fearful thing to fall into the hands of the living God, who has said that He will take vengeance for these things? (Hebrews 10:31.)

> Devouring whales, and ravenous sharks, do follow
> The lesser fry, and at one gulp do swallow
> Some hundreds of them, as our seamen say;
> But we can tell far stranger things than they.
>
> For we have sharks ashore in ev'ry creek,
> Who to devour poor men do hunt and seek.
> No tenderness or pity in them be—
> Nay, have they not cast off humanity?
>
> Extortioners, and cheaters, whom God hates,
> Have dreadful open mouths, and through those gates
> Brave persons with their heritages pass
> In funeral state, friends crying out "Alas!"
>
> O give me Agur's wish,[2] that I may neither
> Be such myself, or feel the hands of either.
> And as for those that feel that evil bite,
> Pity and rescue, Lord, from that sad plight.

---

[2] **Proverbs 30:7-9**

When I behold the squeaking lark that's borne
In falcon's talons, crying, bleeding, torn;
I pity its sad case, and would relieve
The pris'ner, if I could, as well as grieve.

Fountain of pity! Hear the piteous moans
That rise to Thee from captives. Hear the groans
Of all Thy children, sore oppressed, undone,
And rise in judgment for Thy chosen ones.

Chapter Thirteen

Deception and Death

*"Fools make a mock at sin:
but among the righteous there is favour."*

— *Proverbs 14:9*

Despite the successful adventures of Roberts and his crew, it was with great difficulty that they could be kept together under any kind of regulation. For, being almost always mad or drunk, their behavior produced infinite disorders, every man being in his own imagination a captain, a prince, or a king.

When Roberts saw that there was no managing of such a company of wild, ungovernable brutes by gentle means, nor to keep them from drinking to excess—the cause of all their disturbances—he put on a rougher manner and a more magisterial bearing towards them, correcting whom he thought fit. And if any seemed to resent his treatment, he told them "you may go ashore and take satisfaction of me, it you think fit, at sword and pistol, for I neither value nor fear any of you."

About four hundred leagues from the coast of Africa the brigantine, who had up to this time lived with them in all friendly intercourse, thought fit to take the opportunity of a dark night and leave the commodore, which leads me back to the

relation of an accident that happened at one of the islands of the West Indies where they filled their casks with water before they undertook this voyage, which very nearly threw their government (such as it was) off the hinges, and was partly the reason for the separation. The story is as follows:

Captain Roberts, having been insulted by one of the drunken crew (whose name I have forgot), he in the heat of his anger killed the fellow on the spot. This was resented by a great many others, but particularly one Jones, a brisk, active young man (who died lately in the Marshalsea prison), and was his messmate. Jones was at that time ashore a-watering the ship, but as soon as he came on board he was told that Captain Roberts had killed his comrade. At this he cursed Roberts, and said he ought to be treated so himself.

Roberts, hearing Jones' angry speech, ran to him with a sword. He ran him through the body, but Jones, despite his wound, seized the captain, threw him over a cannon, and beat him soundly.

This adventure put the whole company in an uproar. And, as some took part with the captain, and others against him, there came near to being a general battle with one another. However, the tumult was at length quieted by the mediation of the quartermaster.[1] And, as the majority of the company were of opinion that the dignity of the captain ought to be supported on board, that it was a post of honor, and therefore the person whom they thought fit to confer it on should not be injured by any single member, therefore they sentenced Jones to undergo two lashes from every one of the company for his misdemeanor, which was executed upon him as soon as he was well of his wound.

This severe punishment did not at all convince Jones that he was in the wrong, but rather spurred him on to some sort of revenge. But, not being able to do it upon Roberts' person on board the ship, he and several of his comrades plotted with Anstis, captain of the brigantine, and conspired with him and some of the principal pirates on board that vessel to desert from the company. What made Anstis discontented was the inferiority he stood in with respect to Roberts, who acted with a haughty and magisterial air to him and his crew. Roberts regarded the brigantine only as a tender,[2] and, as such, left them nothing more than the worst of the plunder.

In short, Jones and his consort went on board of Captain Anstis' ship under the false appearance of a visit. And there, consulting with their brethren, they found a majority happy to leave Roberts, and so came to a resolution to bid "a soft farewell," as they call it, that night, and to throw overboard whoever should disagree. But they proved to be unanimous, and carried out their plan as above mentioned.

(I shall have no more to say of Captain Anstis till the story of Roberts is concluded. Therefore I return now to Roberts in the pursuit of his voyage to Guinea.)

The loss of the brigantine was a great shock to the crew, for she was an excellent sailer and had seventy hands aboard. However, Roberts, who was the cause of the misfortune, put on a face of unconcern at this his ill conduct and mismanagement, and resolved not to alter his purposes upon that account.

Roberts fell in to windward near the river Senegal. This river is monopolized by the French, who constantly keep cruisers there to hinder the smugglers. At this time they had two small ships in that service, one of ten guns and 65 men and the other of sixteen guns and 75 men who, having got a sight of Mr. Roberts, and supposing him to be one of these prohibited traders, chased him with all the sail

---

[1] **quartermaster** – an officer appointed to assist the ship's master and mates

[2] **tender** – small vessel employed to attend upon a larger one

they could.

But their hopes, which had brought them very close to him, too late deceived them, for on the hoisting of Jolly Roger (the name they give their black flag) their French hearts failed, and they both surrendered without any—or at least very little—resistance. With these prizes the pirates went into Sierra Leone, and made one of the ships their consort by the name of the *Ranger,* and the other a storeship.

In the beginning of January they took the ship called the *King Solomon,* with twenty men in their boat, and a trading vessel. The pirate ship happened to fall about a league to leeward[3] of the *King Solomon,* at Cape Appollonia, and the current and wind opposing their working up with the ship, they agreed to send the longboat with sufficient men to take her.

The pirates are all volunteers on these occasions, the word being always given, "Who will go?" And presently the staunch and firm men offer themselves because by such readiness they display their courage, and have a larger share out of the prize.

---

[3] **leeward** – opposite side from which the wind is blowing

They rowed towards the *King Solomon* with a great deal of cheerful willingness. And, being hailed by the commander of her, they answered defiance. Captain Trahern, before this, observing a great number of men in the boat, began not to like his visitors, and prepared to receive them, firing a musket as they came under his stern, which they returned with a volley, and made greater speed to get on board.

Upon this the captain called to his men, and asked them whether they would stand by him to defend the ship, it being a shame they should be taken by half their number without any defense being offered. But his boatswain,[4] Philips, took upon him to be the mouth of the people, and put an end to the dispute. He said plainly that he would not fight, then laid down his arms in the King's name (as he was pleased to term it), and called out to the boat for quarters,[5] so that the rest by his example were misled to the losing of the ship.

When the pirates came on board they brought her under sail by a speedy method of cutting the anchor's cable. As he did this Walden, one of the pirates, told Captain Trahern that this hope of heaving up the anchor was a needless trouble when they

---

[4] **boatswain** – officer who superintends the sails, rigging, anchors, etc.

[5] **quarters** – to spare the lives of captives or enemies

intended to burn the ship. They brought her under Commodore Roberts' stern, and not only emptied her of what sails, cordage, etc., they wanted for themselves, but wastefully threw the other goods overboard, like squanderers who neither expected or designed any account.

On the same day also they took the *Flushing*, a Dutch ship, robbed her of her masts, yards, and stores, and then cut down her foremast. But what sat as heavily as anything with the skipper was their taking some fine sausages he had on board that his wife had made him. The pirates strung them in a ridiculous manner round their necks till they had sufficiently showed their contempt of them, and then threw them into the sea. Others chopped the heads of his fowls off to be dressed for their supper, and courteously invited the landlord to dine with them, if he promised to find liquor. It was a melancholy request to the man, but it must be complied with, and he was obliged, as they grew drunk, to sit quietly and hear them sing French and Spanish songs out of his Dutch prayer-books, with other profaneness that he, though a Dutchman, stood amazed at.

Hearing of Roberts' plundering and violence, a man-of-war, the *Swallow*, was sent to capture the pirates. While sailing toward Cape Lopez on the 5th of February, the ship heard the report of a gun at dawn. As the day brightened she found that the noise came from Cape Lopez Bay, where she discovered three ships at anchor, the largest with the king's colors and pendant flying, which was soon after concluded to be Mr. Roberts and his consorts.

But, the *Swallow* being to

windward and unexpectedly deep in the bay, was obliged to steer off in order to avoid a sandbar. The pirates, watching the movements of the ship and not knowing her identity, rashly assumed that she was attempting to retreat in fear, and ordered the *Ranger* to chase out in all haste, bending several of their sails in the pursuit.

The man-of-war, finding that the pirates had foolishly mistaken her design, humored the deceit and kept off to sea, as if she had been really afraid, and managed her steerage so under the direction of Lieutenant Sun, an experienced officer, as to let the *Ranger* come up with her when they thought they had got so far away as not to have their guns heard by the other pirates at the Cape. The pirates had such an opinion of their own courage that they could never dream anybody would use a deceitful trick in order to approach them, and so were the more easily drawn into the snare.

The pirates now drew near enough to fire their chase guns. They hoisted the black flag and prepared to board the man-of-war, no one having ever asked all this while what country ship they took the vessel to be. They assumed she was a Portuguese vessel carrying sugar (which they sorely lacked), and were swearing every minute at the wind or sail to speed so sweet a chase. But, alas! All turned sour in an instant.

It was with the utmost astonishment and terror that they saw her suddenly bring-to, now within pistol-shot, and haul up her lower ports, revealing her cannons. Immediately the pirates lowered their black flag. But, after the first surprise was over, they kept firing at a distance, hoisted the flag again, and flourished their cutlasses with boastful bravado, at the same time wisely endeavoring to get away as quickly as they could.

Being now at their wits' end, boarding was proposed by the heads of them, and so to make one desperate push. But, the motion not being well seconded, and their maintop-mast coming down by a shot, after two hours' firing it was declined. The pirates grew sick of the fight, struck their colors,[6] and called out for quarter, having had ten men killed outright and twenty wounded.

Not a single one of the king's men had been lost or hurt. She had 32 guns, manned with sixteen Frenchmen, twenty blacks, and seventy-seven English.

At their surrender the pirates threw their flag overboard, that it might not rise in judgment nor be displayed in triumph over them.

While the *Swallow* was sending their boat to fetch the prisoners, a blast and smoke was seen to pour out of the great cabin on the pirate ship, and they thought they were blowing up. But upon inquiry afterwards they found that half a dozen of the most desperate pirates, when they saw all hopes fled, had drawn themselves round what powder they had left in the steerage[7] and fired a pistol into it in an attempt to blow themselves up. But it was too small a quantity to effect anything more than burning them in a frightful manner.

The men from the man-of-war secured the prisoners with pinions[8] and shackles. The ship was so much disabled in the engagement that they at first decided to set her on fire, but they would then have had the difficulty of transporting all the pirate's wounded men on board themselves. Besides, they were certain that the *Royal Fortune* would wait for their consort's return, and so they lay by her two days, repairing her rigging and other damages, and sent her into Princes with the Frenchmen and four of their own hands.

On the 9th of February, in the evening, the *Swallow* gained the Cape again and saw the *Royal Fortune* standing into the bay with the *Neptune*, a ship they had just captured. The man-of-war looked upon this as a good sign of the next day's success, for they did not doubt that the temptation of liquor and plunder the pirates might find in this their new prize would make them very confused, and so it happened.

On the 10th in the morning the man-of-war bore away to round the Cape. Roberts' crew perceived their masts over the land and went down into the cabin to tell Roberts of it, he being then at breakfast with his new guest, Captain Hill, on a savory dish of Solomon Gundy[9] and some of his own beer. Roberts took no notice of it, and his men almost as little, some saying she was a Portuguese ship, others

---

[6] **struck their colors** – lowered their flag in surrender

[7] **steerage** – area located below the quarterdeck

[8] **pinions** – chains or ropes used to bind the arms

[9] **Solomon Gundy** – a tasty sea dish made of slices of cured fish and onions

a French slave ship, but the major part swore it was the French *Ranger* returning, and were merrily debating for some time on the manner of reception, whether they should salute or not.

But as the *Swallow* approached closer, things appeared plainer, and though any who showed any fear of danger were branded with the name of cowards, yet some of them, now undeceived, declared to Roberts that the ship was a man-of-war, especially one Armstrong, who had deserted from that ship and knew her well. Those Roberts swore at as cowards, who meant to dishearten the men, asking them if it were so, whether they were afraid to fight or no? And he hardly restrained from blows.

What Roberts' own suspicions were till she hauled up her ports and hoisted the king's flag is uncertain. But, being finally perfectly convinced, he slipped his cable,[10] got under sail, and ordered his men to arms without any show of timidity, dropping a first-rate oath, but at the same time resolved like a gallant rogue to get clear or die.

There was one Armstrong, as I just mentioned, a deserter from the *Swallow*, whom they inquired of concerning the trim and sailing of that ship. He told them she sailed best upon a wind, and therefore if they intended to escape from her, they should sail before the wind.

The danger was imminent, and time was very short for Roberts to find a way of escaping. His decision in this difficulty was as follows: To pass close to the *Swallow* with all their sails, and receive her broadside before they returned a shot. If disabled by this, or if they could not depend on sailing, then they would run on shore at the point, and everyone would look out for himself among the natives. Or, if they failed in this, they would board her and blow up together, for he saw that the greatest part of his men were drunk, passively courageous, and unfit for service.

---

[10] **slipped his cable** – left quickly by leaving the cable without taking time to weigh the anchor

Deception and Death

Roberts himself made a gallant figure at the time of the engagement, being dressed in a rich crimson silk waistcoat and breeches, a red feather in his hat, a gold chain round his neck, with a diamond cross hanging to it, a sword in his hand, and two pairs of pistols hanging at the end of a silk sling flung over his shoulders (according to the fashion of the pirates). He is said to have given his orders with boldness and spirit.

Following his plan Roberts drew close to the man-of-war, received her fire, and then hoisted his black flag and fired his own guns while sailing away from her with all the sail he could pack. And, had he taken Armstrong's advice to have gone before the wind, he would probably have escaped. But, keeping his tacks down, either by the wind shifting or ill steerage, or both, he was taken aback with his sails, and the *Swallow* came a second time very near to him.

Roberts would now probably have finished the fight very desperately if death, who took a swift passage in a grape-shot,[11] had not interposed and struck him directly on the throat. He settled himself on the tackles of a gun, which one Stephenson observing, ran to his assistance. And, not perceiving him wounded, Stephenson swore at him and bid him stand up and fight like a man. But when he found his mistake, and that his captain was certainly dead, he burst into tears and wished the next shot might take his life, also.

The pirates immediately threw Roberts overboard, with his weapons and ornaments on, according to the repeated requests he had made in his lifetime. When Roberts was gone, as though he had been the life and soul of the gang, their spirits sank. Many deserted their posts, and all stupidly neglected any means for defense or escape. And, their main-mast soon after being struck and falling over the ship's side, they had no way left but to surrender and call for quarter.

The *Swallow* kept her distance while her boat passed and repassed for the prisoners because they understood that the pirates were under an oath to blow up their ship. And some of the desperadoes showed a willingness that way, matches being lighted and scuffles happening between those who would and those who opposed it. But I cannot easily account for this action, which can be termed no more than a false courage, since any of them had power to destroy his own life either by pistol or drowning, without involving others in the same fate who are in no temper of mind for it. And, at best, it would only be dying for fear of death.

The *Royal Fortune* had forty guns and 157 men, forty-five of whom were

---

[11] **grape-shot** – a cluster of small shot used in cannon

blacks; three only were killed in the action, without any loss to the *Swallow*. There was found upwards of £2,000 in gold dust in her. The *Royal Fortune's* flag could not be easily gotten from under the fallen mast, and was therefore recovered by the *Swallow*. It had the figure of a skeleton in it, and a man portrayed with a flaming sword in his hand, suggesting a defiance of death itself.

As to the pirates' behavior after they were taken, it was found that they had great desires to rebel if they could have laid hold of any opportunity, for they were very uneasy under restraint, having been lately all commanders themselves, nor could they endure their diet or quarters without cursing and swearing and upbraiding each other with the folly that had brought them to it.

Yet even in these circumstances most of the pirates remained impenitent and wicked. One of them, Sutton, was a very profane man, and happened to be chained with another prisoner who was more serious than ordinary. This man read and prayed often, as was appropriate for his condition, but Sutton would swear at him and ask:

"What do you seek by so much noise and devotion?"

"Heaven," says the other, "I hope."

"Heaven? You fool!" says Sutton. "Did you ever hear of any pirates going there? Give me hell! It's a merrier place! I'll give Roberts a salute of thirteen guns at entrance!"

But when Sutton discovered that such foolish expressions caused no change in his companion, he made a formal complaint to the ship's officer, and requested that he would either remove this man or take his Prayer Book away, for he declared that he was a disturber of the peace.

"Fools make a mock at sin:
but among the righteous there is favour."

— *Proverbs 14:9*

Chapter Fourteen

Creatures from the Deep

Within these smooth-faced seas strange creatures crawl,
But in man's heart, far stranger than them all.

It was a foolish saying of Plato when he declared: "the sea produces nothing memorable." To the contrary, surely there is much of the wisdom, power, and goodness of God revealed in those inhabitants of the watery region.

Despite the sea's blue and smiling face, strange creatures are bred in its womb. As David says, "O Lord, how manifold are Thy works? In wisdom hast Thou made them all. The earth is full of Thy riches. So is this great and wide sea, wherein are things creeping innumerable, both small and great beasts" (Psalm 104:24-25). And we read in Lamentations 4:3 of sea monsters which offer their breasts to their young. Around the tropic of Capricorn our seamen meet with flying fishes that have wings of a silver color; they fly in

flocks. How strange, both in shape and makeup, is the sword-fish and thresher, that fight with the whale? Even our own seas produce creatures of strange shapes, but the commonness of them takes off the wonder.

Application

Even as the ocean abounds with strange creatures, so also does the heart of man naturally swarm and abound with strange and monstrous lusts and abominations. Man's heart is "filled with all unrighteousness, fornication, wickedness,

covetousness, maliciousness,¹ full of envy, murder, debate, deceit, malignity,² whisperers, backbiters, haters of God, despiteful, proud, boasters, inventors of evil things, disobedient to parents, without understanding, covenant-breakers, without natural affection, implacable,³ unmerciful" (Romans 1:29-31).

    O what a swarm of nasty creatures is here! And yet there are multitudes more in the depths of the heart! And it is no wonder, considering that with this nature we received the seed of the blackest and vilest abominations. This original lust is able to produce them all (James 1:14-15). And, though this lust may show itself in a different *number* of sins in every man, yet it is but one and the same *substance,* according to its sort and kind, in all the children of Adam. It is the same as the soul. For, though every man has his own soul—that is, he possesses a soul individually distinct from another man's—yet it is the same *kind* of soul in all men.

    Therefore whatever abominations are in the hearts and lives of the most wicked Sodomites and most evil and indecent wretches under heaven, there is the

---

[1] **maliciousness** – wickedness

[2] **malignity** – unjust hatred, evilness of nature

[3] **implacable** – stubbornly unforgiving

same matter in your heart out of which they were shaped and formed. In the depths of the heart they are conceived, and from thence they crawl out of the eyes, hands, lips, and all other members of the body. As Christ says, "Those things which proceed out of the mouth, come forth from the heart, and defile a man. For out of the heart proceed evil thoughts, murders, adulteries, fornications, thefts, false witness, blasphemies" (Matthew 15:18-19).

Ah, such monsters as these are would make a gracious heart tremble to behold! "What are my lusts," (says one) "but so many toads spitting of venom, and breeding poison; croaking in my judgment, creeping in my will, and crawling in my desires?" The apostle tells of a sin not even to be named (in 1 Corinthians 5:1). So monstrous is it that nature itself is startled at the sight of it. Even such monsters are generated in the depths of the heart.

From where do these evils come? This was a question that much puzzled the philosophers of old, but from these Scriptures you may see where they come from, and where they are begotten.

REFLECTION

And are there such strange abominations in the heart of man? Then how greatly has he fallen from his original perfection and glory! His streams were once as clear as crystal, and the fountain of them pure; there was no unclean creature moving in them. What a stately fabric was the soul at first! And what holy inhabitants possessed its many rooms! But now (as God speaks of Idumea), "The line of confusion is stretched out upon it, and the stones of emptiness; the cormorant and bittern possess it; the owl and the raven dwell in it" (Isaiah 34:11). Yes, the wild beasts of the desert lie there, and it is full of dismal creatures. The satyrs dance in it, and dragons cry in those once pleasant places (Isaiah 13:21-22).

O sad change! How sadly may we look back towards our first state and take up the words of Job, "O that I were as in months past, as in the days of my youth; when the Almighty was yet with me, when I put on righteousness and it clothed me, when my glory was fresh in me" (Job 29:2-14).

Again, think, O my soul, what a miserable condition the unregenerate abide in! They are swarming and over-run with hellish lusts, under the dominion and subjection of so many lusts (Titus 3:3). What a tumultuous sea is such a soul!

How greatly do these lusts rage within them! How violently do they struggle and battle for the throne! And usually they take it one after another. For, as all diseases are contrary to health, yet some contrary to each other, so are lusts. Hence poor creatures are hurried on to different kinds of slavery according to the nature of that ruling lust that is on the throne. And, like the demon-possessed man in Matthew 17, they are sometimes cast into the water and sometimes into the fire.

Well might the prophet say, "The wicked is like the troubled sea that cannot rest" (Isaiah 57:20). They have no peace now in the slavery of sin, and less they shall have hereafter when they receive the wages of sin. "There is no peace, saith the LORD, unto the wicked" (Isaiah 48:22). They indeed cry "Peace, peace!" but my God does not say so. The last end and result of this is eternal death. No sooner is the soul delivered from its deceitful pleasures than it immediately falls in travail again, and brings forth death (James 1:15).

Let us consider one more thing. Is the heart such a sea, abounding with monstrous abominations? Then stand astonished, O my soul, at that free grace which has delivered you from so sad a condition. O fall down, and kiss the feet of mercy that came so freely and timely to your rescue! Let my heart be enlarged abundantly here.

Lord, what am I, that I should be taken, and others left? Reflect, O my soul, upon the conceptions and births of lusts in the days of vanity, which you blush and are ashamed to admit of. O what black imaginations, hellish desires, and vile passions are lodged there! Who made me to differ from the wickedest of men? Or how came I to be thus wonderfully separated to the salvation of God? Surely it is by Your free grace, O Lord, and nothing else. This is why I am what I am. And by that grace I have escaped (to my own amazement) the corruption that is in the world through lust. O what a wonder it is that the holy God should ever set His eyes on such a one as me, or cast a look of love towards me, in whom were legions of unclean lusts and abominations!

> My soul's the sea, in which, from day to day,
> Sins, like leviathans, do sport and play.
> Great master-lusts, with all the lesser fry,
> Do there increase, and strangely multiply.

Yet it's not strange that sin so fast should breed,
Since with my nature I received the seed.
And in my heart the seed of ev'ry sin
Is birthed and nourished carefully within.

By its own warmth, my soul, just like the sun,
Enlivens them, and now abroad they come.
And, like the frogs of Egypt, creep and crawl
Into the closest rooms within the soul.

My thoughts do swarm, for there they frisk and play
In dreams by night and foolishness by day.
My judgment's clouded by them, and my will
Perverted; every corner they do fill.

As locusts seize on all that's fresh and green,
Devour the beauteous spring, and make it seem
Like drooping autumn, so my soul, that first
As Eden seemed, now's like a ground that's cursed.

Lord, purge my streams, and kill those lusts that lie
Within me. If they do not, I must die.

Captain Anstis

Chapter Fifteen

A Divided Band of Pirates

*"Lo, this only have I found,
that God hath made man upright;
but they have sought out many inventions."*

— *Ecclesiastes 7:29*

Thomas Anstis shipped himself at Providence in the year 1718 aboard the *Buck* sloop, and was one of six that conspired together to go off a-pirating with the vessel. The other five were Howel Davis (Roberts' predecessor, killed at the Island of Princes), Dennis Topping (killed at the taking of the rich Portuguese ship on the coast of Brazil), Walter Kennedy (hanged at Execution Dock), and two others whose names I will not mention, because I understand that they are at this day employed in an honest occupation in this city.

What followed concerning Anstis' piracies has been included in the preceding chapters. I shall only observe that the combination of these six men abovementioned was the beginning of that company that afterwards proved so formidable under Captain Roberts. Anstis deserted from him the 18th of April, 1721, in the

brigantine *Good Fortune,* leaving his Commodore to pursue his piracies upon the coast of Guinea, while Anstis returned to the West Indies upon the same errand.

About the middle of June these pirates met with one Captain Marston, bound on a voyage to New York. From him they took all the clothing they could find, as well as his liquors and provision, and five of his men, but did not touch his cargo. Two or three other vessels were also plundered by them in this cruise, out of whom they stocked themselves with provisions and men. Among the rest, I think, was the *Irwin,* Captain Ross' ship. This ship had 600 barrels of beef aboard, besides other provisions, and was taken off Martinique, in which Colonel Doyly and his family were passengers.

The Colonel was very much abused and wounded for attempting to save a poor woman that was also a passenger from the insults of that beastly crew. But the pirates prevailed, and abused and murdered the poor woman.

When the pirates thought fit to put an end to this cruise, they went into one of the islands to clean, which they carried out without any disturbance, and came out again and stretching away towards Bermuda, met with a stout ship called the *Morning Star* bound from Guinea to Carolina. They made a prize of her and kept her for their own use.

In a day or two a ship from Barbados (bound to New York) fell into their hands. And, taking out her guns and tackle, they mounted the *Morning Star* with thirty-two pieces of cannon, manned her with a hundred men, and appointed a man by the name of John Fenn as Captain. The brigantine was of far less force, so the *Morning Star* should have fallen to Anstis, as elder officer, but he was so in love with his own vessel (she being an excellent sailer) that he chose to stay in her and let Fenn, who was before his gunner, command the great ship.

Now that they had two good ships well manned, it may be supposed that they were in a condition to undertake something bold. But their piratical government was disturbed by discontented fellows, and a kingdom divided against itself cannot stand (Luke 11:17). They had a great number of new men among them who seemed not so violently inclined for the game. So it was that, whatever the Captain proposed, they almost certainly voted against him, so that they came to no agreement at all in trying to decide what to do. Therefore  there was nothing to be done but to break up the company, which seemed to be the inclination of the majority. But the manner of doing so concerned their common safety; to which purpose various means were suggested.

It was finally concluded that they would send home a petition to his Majesty asking for a pardon, and await his response. At the same time Jones (one of the pirates), the boatswain of the *Good Fortune*, suggested a place of safe retreat, which was an uninhabited island near Cuba.

This suggestion was approved of and unanimously agreed to. Then a petition was drawn up and signed by the whole company in the manner of what they call a *round robin*—that is, all the names were written in a circle in order to avoid all appearance of pre-eminence, and lest any person should be marked out by the government as a principal rogue among them.

The Petition

To his most sacred Majesty King George, by the Grace of God, of Great Britain, France and Ireland, King, Defender of the Faith, etc.

The humble petition of the company now belonging to the ship Morning Star and brigantine Good Fortune, lying under the shameful name and denomination of PIRATES, humbly shows,

That we, your Majesty's most loyal subjects, have at certain times been taken by Bartholomew Roberts, the former captain of the before-mentioned vessels and company, together with another ship (in which we left him). And we have been forced

EXAMPLE OF A ROUND ROBIN

by him and his wicked accomplices to enter into and serve in the same company as pirates, though much contrary to our wills and inclinations.

And we, your loyal subjects, utterly abhorring and detesting that ungodly way of living, did unanimously consent (contrary to the knowledge of Captain Roberts or his accomplices), on or about the 18th day of April, 1721, and did leave and run away with the ship Morning Star and the brigantine Good Fortune, with no other intent and meaning than the hopes of obtaining your Majesty's most gracious pardon.

A Divided Band of Pirates

And, in order that we your Majesty's most loyal subjects may safely return to our native country and serve the nation to which we belong without fear of being prosecuted by those we have injured, whose estates have suffered by Captain Roberts and his accomplices while we were forcibly detained among them, we most humbly implore your Majesty's most royal assent to this our humble petition.

This petition was sent home by a merchant ship bound to England, who promised to meet with the petitioners about twenty leagues to windward of that island at their return and let them know what success their petition met with.

When this was done the pirates retired to the island with the ship and brigantine. Here they stayed about nine months. But, having provisions for only about two months, they were forced to take what the island supplied, which was fish of several sorts—particularly turtle, which was the main food they lived on, and was found in great plenty on the coasts of this island. Whether there were any wild hogs, beef, or other cattle common to several islands of the West Indies, or whether the pirates were too lazy to hunt them, I know not. But I was informed by them that, for the whole time they lived there, they ate no meat except turtle.

The pirates passed their time here in dancing and other festivities agreeable to these sort of folks. And among other games they held a mock trial, to try one another for piracy, and he that was a criminal one day was made judge another.

I had an account given me of one of these merry trials, and as it appeared amusing, I shall give the readers a short account of it:

The court and criminals being both

appointed, as also council to plead, the Judge got up into a tree and had a dirty tarpaulin[1] hung over his shoulders. This was used instead of a robe, with a coarse woolen cap on his head and a large pair of spectacles upon his nose. Thus equipped, he settled himself in his place, with an abundance of officers attending him below.

The criminals were brought out, making a thousand sour faces, and one who acted as attorney general opened the charge against them. Their speeches were very brief, and their whole proceedings short. We shall give it as a dialogue:

Attorney General: "An't please your lordship, and you gentlemen of the jury, here is a fellow before you that is a sad dog, a sad, sad dog. And I humbly hope your lordship will order him to be hanged out of the way immediately.

"He has committed piracy upon the high seas, and we shall prove, an't please your lordship, that this fellow, this sad dog before you, has escaped a thousand storms—nay, has got safe ashore when the ship has been cast away, which is a certain sign that he was not born to be drowned.

"Yet, not having the fear of hanging before his eyes, he went on robbing and ravishing man, woman, and child, plundering ship's cargoes fore and aft, burning and sinking ship, vessel, and boat, as if the devil had been in him.

"My lord, I should have spoken much finer than I do now, but, as your lordship knows, our rum is all out, and how can a man speak good law that has not drunk a dram?[2] However, I hope your lordship will order the fellow to be hanged."

---

[1] **tarpaulin** – canvas covered with tar to render it waterproof

[2] **dram** – a serving of liquor

Judge: "Hearkee me, sirrah—you lousy, pitiful, ill-lookin' dog. What have you to say why you should not be tucked up immediately and set a-sun-drying like a scare-crow? Are you guilty or not guilty?"

Prisoner: "Not guilty, an't please your worship."

Judge: "Not guilty! Say so again, sirrah, and I'll have you hanged without any trial!"

Prisoner: "An't please your worship's honor, my lord, I am as honest a poor fellow as ever went between stem and stern of a ship. I can hand, reef, steer, and clap two ends of a rope together as well as ever a man that crossed salt water. But I was taken by George Bradley (the name of the man that sat as 'Judge'), a notorious pirate, as sad a rogue as ever was unhanged, and he forced me to turn pirate, an't please your honor."

Judge: "Answer me, sirrah. How will you be tried?"

Prisoner: "By God and my country."

Judge: "Why then, gentlemen of the jury, I think we have nothing to do but to proceed to judgment."

Attorney General: "Right, my lord. For if the fellow should be permitted to speak, he may clear himself, and that's an affront to the court."

Prisoner: "Pray, my lord, I hope your lordship will consider—"

Judge: "Consider! How dare you talk of considering? Sirrah, sirrah, I never considered in all my life. I'll make it treason to consider."

Prisoner: "But I hope your lordship will hear some reason."

Judge: "D'ye hear how the scoundrel goes on? What have we to do with reason? I'd have you to know, rascal, we don't sit here to hear reason. We go according to law. Is our dinner ready?"

Attorney General: "Yes, my lord."

Judge: "Then heark'ee, you rascal. Hear me, sirrah, hear me. You must suffer for three reasons: first, because it is not fit I should sit here as judge and nobody be hanged.

"Secondly, you must be hanged because you have a hanging look.

"And thirdly, you must be hanged because I am hungry. For know, sirrah, that 'tis a custom that, whenever the judge's dinner is ready before the trial is over, the prisoner is to be hanged of course. There's law for you, ye dog. So take him away, jailer!"

This is the trial just as it was told me. The reason of my setting it down is only to show how these fellows can jest of things whose fear and dread should make them tremble.

The beginning of August, 1722, the pirates made ready the brigantine, and set out to sea to see what had become of their petition. And, beating up to windward, they lay in the track for their correspondent in her voyage to Jamaica and spoke with her. But, finding nothing was done in England in their favor (as 'twas expected), they returned to their companions at the island with the ill news. Thus they found themselves under the necessity (as they supposed) to continue that abominable course of life they had lately practiced.

To carry out this plan they sailed with the ship and brigantine to the southward. But, the next night, by intolerable neglect, they ran the *Morning Star* aground on an island and wrecked her. The brigantine, seeing the fate of her companion ship, hauled off in time, and so avoided the island.

The next day Captain Anstis put in, and found that all or the greatest part of the crew were safe ashore. Therefore he brought the ship to an anchor in order to fetch them off. And, having brought Fenn the captain, Philips the carpenter, and a few others aboard, two men-of-war suddenly came down upon them (the *Hector* and *Adventure*). The brigantine had but just time to cut their cable and get to sea, with one of the men-of-war after her, keeping within gun-shot for several hours.

Anstis and his crew were now under the greatest consternation imaginable, finding the winds picking up and the man-of-war gaining ground upon them, so that in all probability they must have been prisoners in two hours more. But it pleased God to give them a little longer time, and the wind died away and the pirates got out their oars and rowed for their lives, and thereby got clear of their enemy.

The *Hector* landed her men upon the island and took forty of the *Morning Star's* crew, who offered no resistance, but on the contrary declared that they had been forced to remain with the pirates, and were glad of this opportunity to escape from them. The rest hid themselves in the woods and could not be found. George Bradley, the master, and three more surrendered afterwards to a Bermuda sloop, and were carried to that island.

The brigantine, after her escape, sailed to a small island near the Bay of Honduras. And in her way there she took a Rhode Island sloop, Captain Durfey, commander, and two or three other vessels, which they destroyed, but brought all the men aboard their own.

While Anstis was cleaning his ship a scheme was agreed upon between Captain Durfey, some other prisoners, and two or three of the pirates, to seize some of the chief men and carry off the brigantine. But this plot was discovered before the ship was fit for sailing, and thus their plan was prevented. However, Captain Durfey and four or five more got ashore with some arms and ammunition. And, when the pirates' canoe came in for water, he seized the boat with the men. At this Anstis ordered another boat to be manned with thirty hands and sent ashore, which was accordingly done. But Captain Durfey and the company he had by that time got together, gave them such a warm reception that they were contented to flee themselves to their vessel again.

About the beginning of December, 1722, Anstis left this place and returned to the islands, planning to accumulate all the power and strength he could, since there was no looking back. During this cruise he took a good ship commanded by Captain Smith, which he mounted with twenty-four guns. Fenn, a one-handed man (who commanded the *Morning Star* when she was lost), went aboard to command her.

They cruised together and took a vessel or two, and then went to the Bahama Islands and there met with what they wanted, that is, a sloop loaded with provisions from Dublin, called the *Antelope*.

It was time now to think of some

place to fit up and clean the frigate they had recently captured, and put her in a condition to do business. Accordingly they decided upon the island of Tobago, where they arrived the beginning of April, 1723, with the *Antelope* and her cargo.

The pirates fell to work immediately, got the guns, stores, and everything else out upon the island, and put the ship upon the heel.³ And just then, as "ill luck" would have it, the man-of-war *Winchelsea* came in by way of visit, which put the marooners into such a surprise that they set fire to the ship and sloop and fled ashore to the woods.

Anstis in the brigantine, escaped by having a light pair of heels, but it put his company into such a disorder that their government could never be set to rights again. For some of the newcomers and those who had been tired with the trade put an end to the reign by shooting Thomas Anstis in his hammock. And afterwards

they put the quartermaster and two or three others into irons. The rest submitted, and they surrendered them and the vessel, at Curacao, a Dutch settlement, where they were tried and hanged; and those concerned in delivering up the vessel were acquitted.

> *"Lo, this only have I found,*
> *that God hath made man upright;*
> *but they have sought out many inventions."*
>
> — *Ecclesiastes 7:29*

---

³ **upon the heel** – to lay (a ship) upon its side

Chapter Sixteen

The Leak that Sank the Ship

Neglect a little leak; disaster comes.
So let but one sin live, and you're undone.

The smallest leak, if not discovered and stopped in time, is enough to sink the greatest ship. Therefore seamen are accustomed to frequently measure what water is in the hold. And, if they find it entering in and increasing upon them, they man the pump and presently set the carpenters to search for the leak and stop it. And, until it be found, they have no rest.

Application

What such a leak is to a ship, so is the smallest sin, neglected, to the soul. One sin is enough to ruin it eternally. For, as the greatest sin discovered, lamented, and mourned over by a believer cannot ruin him, so the least sin, if it be indulged in, covered up, and concealed, will certainly prove the destruction of the sinner. No sin, though never so small, is tolerated

by the pure and perfect law of God (Psalm 119:96). "The command is exceeding broad," not as though it gives men room to walk as they please, but *broad*, that is, extending itself to *all* our words, thoughts, actions, and desires. It lays a law upon them all, and allows no evil whatever in any man (1 Peter 2:1).

And, as the word gives no allowance for the least sin, so it is the very nature of sincerity and uprightness to set the heart against every way of wickedness (Psalm 139:23-24; Job 4:23), and especially against that sin which was its delight in the days of his vanity (Psalm 18:23). True hatred is of the whole kind: he that hates sin as sin (as does every upright soul) hates *all* sins as well as *some*.

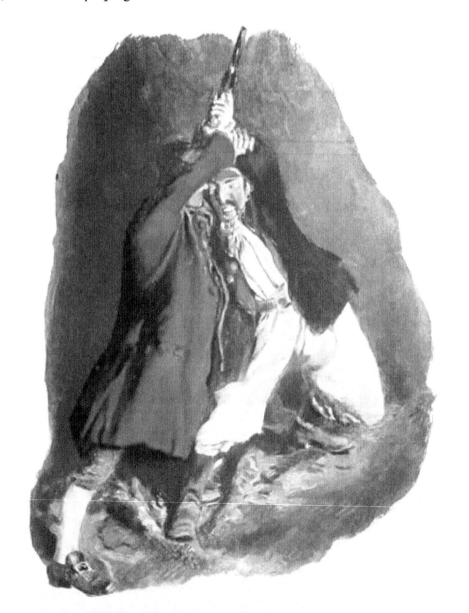

Again, the soul that has had a saving sight of Jesus Christ and a true understanding of the evil of sin by gazing into the mirror both of the law and the gospel, can look upon no sin as a small matter. He knows that the punishment even the smallest sin deserves is God's eternal wrath, and that not even the least sin can be forgiven without the shedding and application of the blood of Christ (Hebrews 9:22), whose blood is of infinite value and price (1 Peter 1:19).

To conclude, God's people know that both little and great sins are dangerous, deadly, and destructive in their own nature. Even a little poison will destroy a man. A man would think Adam's sin had been no great matter; yet what dreadful work did it make! It was not as a single bullet that killed himself only, but as a chain-shot[1] which cut off all his poor miserable posterity. Indeed, no sin can be little, because God, against whom it is committed, is so great. From this it receives a kind of infiniteness in itself, and because the price paid to redeem us from it is so precious beyond measure.

REFLECTION

And is the smallest sin not only damning in its own nature, but will certainly prove the ruin of that soul that hides and covers it? O then, let my spirit undertake a diligent search. Look to it, O my soul! Let no sin be indulged by you. Set these considerations, as so many flaming swords, in the way of your carnal delights and lusts.

Let me never say of any sin, as Lot did of Zoar, "It is a little one; spare it." Shall I spare that which cost the blood of Jesus Christ? The Lord would not spare it when He made His soul an

---

[1] **chain-shot** – two balls connected by a chain, fired from a cannon, and used to cut down masts or rigging of an enemy's ship

offering for sin (Romans 8:32). Neither will He spare me, if I defend and hide it (Deuteronomy 19:20).

Ah! if my heart were right and my actions sound, that lust, whatever it be, that is so favored by me, would be especially abhorred and hated (Isaiah 2:20, 30:22). Whatever my convictions and reformations have been, yet if there be but one sin retained and delighted in, this keeps the devil's interest still in my soul. And though for a time he seems to depart, yet at last he will return with seven worse spirits, and this is the sin that will open the door to him and deliver up my soul (Matthew 12:43-44).

Lord, let me make a thorough work of sin. Let me cut it off and pluck it out, though it be as a right hand or eye. Ah! Shall I come so near the Kingdom of God and make such a fair declaration for Christ, and yet stick at a small matter, and lose all for want of one thing? Lord, let me shed the blood of my dearest lust, for His sake that shed His dearest blood for me!

> There's many a soul eternally undone
> For sparing sin, because a little one.
> But we are much deceived. No sin is small
> That wounds so great a God, so dear a soul.
>
> Yet, though it were, the smallest penknife may,
> As well as sword or lance, murder and slay.
> And shall so small a matter cut and sever
> Christ and your soul? What! make you part for ever?
>
> Or will you keep such foolish things, when He
> Denied Himself in greatest things for thee?
> Or will it be an ease in hell to think
> How easily your soul therein did sink?
>
> Are Christ and hell for trifles sold and bought?
> Strike souls with trembling, Lord, at such a thought!
> By little sins, beloved, the soul is lost,
> Unless such sins do great repentance cost.

Captain Phillips and his Crew

Chapter Seventeen

Partners in Piracy

"How have I hated instruction, and my heart despised reproof;
and have not obeyed the voice of my teachers,
nor inclined mine ear to them that instructed me!
I was almost in all evil
in the midst of the congregation and assembly."

— Proverbs 5:12-14

John Phillips was raised a carpenter and, sailing to Newfoundland in a west-country ship, was taken by Anstis in the *Good Fortune* brigantine the next day after he had left his consort and commodore, Captain Roberts. Phillips was soon reconciled to the life of a pirate, and being a brisk fellow, was appointed carpenter of the vessel (for at first his ambition reached no higher). There he remained till they broke up at Tobago, and was one of those

who came home in a sloop that we have mentioned to be sunk in Bristol Channel.

His stay was not long in England, for while he was paying his first visits to his friends in Devonshire, he heard of the misfortune of some of his companions—that is, of their being taken and committed to Bristol Jail. And, there being good reason for his suspecting danger from a wind that blew from the same quarter, he moved off immediately to Topsham, the nearest port, and there hired himself to one Captain Wadham for a voyage to Newfoundland, and home again. (Which, by the way, Mr. Phillips never intended to perform, or to see England anymore.)

When the ship came to Peter Harbor in Newfoundland, he ran away from her and hired himself in the fishery for the season. But this was only till he could have an opportunity of carrying out his intended rogueries; in order to which he conspired with several others in the same employ, and plotted to steal one of the vessels that lay in the harbor, and set out upon the piratical account. Accordingly the time was fixed: the 29th of August, 1723, at night.

But whether remorse or fear prevented the men from coming together, I know not, but of sixteen men that were in the conspiracy, five only kept the appointment. In spite of this, Phillips voted for pushing forward with that small number, assuring his companions that they should soon increase their company. And, they agreeing, a vessel was seized on, and out of the harbor they sailed.

The first thing they had now to do was to choose officers, draw up articles, and settle their little commonwealth to prevent disputes and wrangling afterwards. So John Phillips was made captain; John Nutt, master (or navigator) of the vessel; James Sparks, gunner; Thomas Fern, carpenter; and William White was the only private crewman in the whole crew.

When this was done, one of them wrote out the following articles (which we have taken word for word) and all the pirates swore to 'em upon a hatchet for lack of a Bible:

The Articles on Board the Revenge

1. Every man shall obey civil command. The Captain shall have one full share and a half in all prizes. The master, carpenter, boatswain,[1] and gunner shall have one share and a quarter.

2. If any man shall attempt to desert or keep any secret from the company, he shall be marooned with one bottle of powder, one bottle of water, one small arm,[2] and shot.

3. If any man shall steal anything in the company, or game, to the value of a piece of eight, he shall be marooned or shot. . . .

Thus prepared, this bold crew set out, and before they left the banks they made prize of several small fishing vessels, out of which they got a few men, some French and some English, and then sailed for the West Indies.

In one of these vessels they took out one John Rose Archer who, having been a pirate under the famous Blackbeard, was immediately preferred over other people's heads to be quartermaster to the company. This sudden promotion so disgusted some of the older standers (especially Fern, the carpenter), that it occasioned some mischief to follow, as we shall show shortly.

The pirates came off Barbados the beginning of October, and cruised there and among other islands about three months without speaking with a vessel, so that they were almost starved for lack of food. They were at last reduced to a pound of meat a day between ten men. At last they fell in with a Martinique ship of twelve guns and 35 hands, far superior in force.

The pirates would not have dared to attack it at another time, but hunger will break down stone walls. They were resolved to show the Frenchmen their

---

[1] **boatswain** – officer who superintends the sails, rigging, anchors, etc.

[2] **small arm** – musket, pistol, or similar weapon

black flag, and if that would not do, they must seek out elsewhere. Accordingly they boldly ran up alongside of the sloop with their piratical colors flying, and told them that if they did not surrender immediately, they would give them no quarters. This so intimidated the Frenchmen that they never fired a gun. This proved a timely supply. They took her provisions and four of her men, and let her go.

In a few days they took a snow[3] with a few hands, and Fern the carpenter, William Phillips, Wood, and Taylor went aboard to take possession of her. Fern, not forgetting the disgrace of having Archer preferred before him, resolved to steal the prize and make off with her. He confided his design to the others, who agreed to go along with him. However, John Phillips the captain, keeping a good lookout, perceived their intention and chased them. Then, coming up with the vessel, a skirmish ensued, in which Wood was killed and Taylor wounded in his leg. At this the other two surrendered.

There was no surgeon aboard, and therefore it was advised, upon a learned consultation, that Taylor's wounded leg should be cut off. But who should perform the operation was the dispute. At length the carpenter was appointed as the most proper man. He therefore fetched up his biggest saw and, taking the limb under his arm, fell to work, and separated the leg from the body of the patient in as little time as he could have cut a board in two. After that he heated his axe red-hot in the fire and cauterized the wound. But this was not done with as much skill as he performed the other part, for he so burnt the flesh distant from the place of amputation that it had like to have mortified. However, nature performed a cure at last without any other assistance.

From Tobago they sailed away to the northward and took a Portuguese ship bound for Brazil and two or three sloops from Jamaica. In one of these Fern the carpenter, again trying to make off with it, was killed by Phillips the Captain, in

[3] **snow** – a two-masted vessel

accordance with their articles. Another man endured the same fate some days afterward for a similar attempt. These severities made it dangerous for any to consult or plan an escape. The terror of this made several men sign the pirates' articles and sit down quietly, waiting impatiently for redemption, which as yet they saw no great likelihood of.

On the 25th of March they took two ships from Virginia heading for London. John Phillips, the pirate captain's namesake, was master of one, and Captain Robert Mortimer, the other, a brisk young fellow who deserved a better fate than he met with. Phillips the pirate stayed on board of Captain Mortimer's ship while they transported the crew to the sloop. And, the boat returning alongside, one of the pirates in it calls to Phillips, and told him that there was a mutiny aboard their vessel: Mortimer had two men in his ship, and the pirate captain had two. Therefore Mortimer thought it a good opportunity to recover his ship, and quickly took up a handspike[4] and struck Phillips over the head, giving him a dangerous wound, but not knocking him down. Phillips recovered and wounded Mortimer with his sword. Then the two pirates that were aboard came to Captain Phillips's assistance, and Captain Mortimer was presently cut to pieces, while his own two men stood by and did nothing.

This was the first voyage that Mortimer had the command of a vessel, and by his death a poor bereaved, sorrowful widow and her poor children are made miserable.

---
[4] **handspike** – wooden bar

This affair ended without any other consequence than a strict search for a brother of Captain Mortimer who was on board, in order to have put him likewise to death. But he had the good fortune to meet with a townsman among the crew, who hid him for four and twenty hours in a sail until the heat of their fury was over. By this means he happily escaped the fate intended for him.

Out of the other Virginia ship before spoken of they took one Edward Cheeseman, a carpenter, to supply the place of their dead carpenter Fern. Cheeseman was a modest, sober young man, very opposed to their unlawful occupation, and a brave, gallant fellow.

John Philmore, one of the men previously taken by the pirates, was ordered to row Cheeseman aboard of Mortimer's ship, which the pirates took possession of. Philmore, seeing with what reluctance and uneasiness Cheeseman was brought away, told him that he would join with him in some plan to overthrow the piratical government. He told him of their present condition, and what difficulties Phillips had met with to make up his company, and how few voluntary pirates there were on board.

But, however plausible this seemed, Cheeseman (out of caution) rejected Philmore's offers of assistance till he saw some proofs of his sincerity. After a few days he was convinced of his honesty, and then they often consulted together. But, as the old pirates were always suspicious of the newcomers and closely watched their behavior, Cheeseman and Philmore took great caution when they discussed their plans. They plotted mostly when they were lying down together, as though asleep. And at other times they talked when they were playing at cards; both which they pretended often to do for that purpose.

The pirates went on all the while, plundering and robbing several ships and vessels, bending their course towards Newfoundland, where they intended to raise more men and do all the mischief they could on the banks and in the harbors.

The 14th of April they took a sloop belonging to Cape Ann, with Andrew Harradine as master. They looked upon this vessel as more fit for their purpose, and so came aboard, keeping only her master and sending Harradine's crew away in Salter's vessel, which they till this time had detained. Cheeseman the carpenter revealed his plans to Harradine, and brought him into the confederacy to destroy the crew, and the plot was put into execution four days afterwards.

Harradine and the rest voted for doing the business in the night because

they believed the crew would be more easily caught off guard. This was because Nut, the master, was a fellow of great strength and no less courage, and it was thought dangerous to attack him without firearms. However, Cheeseman was determined to perform it by daylight, because there would then be less likelihood of confusion. And, as to the master, he offered to lay hands on him first.

At this 'twas concluded on, twelve o'clock noon being the appointed time. Cheeseman, in preparation for the business, left his carpenter's tools on the deck as though he had been going to use them, and walked aft.[5] But perceiving some signs of fear in Harradine, he came back, fetched his brandy bottle, and gave him and the rest a dram.[6] Then he takes a walk along the ship's deck with Nut, asking what he thought of the weather, and such like.

In the meanwhile Philmore takes up the axe and twirls it around, as though playing with it. Then both he and Harradine wink at Cheeseman, letting him know they were ready.

At this signal Cheeseman seizes Nut by the collar, with one hand between his legs, and tossed him over the side of the vessel. But Nut, holding on to Cheeseman's sleeve, said, "What are you going to do, carpenter?"

Cheeseman told him it was an unnecessary question. "For," says he, "Master, you are a dead man." He then strikes him over the arm, Nut loses his hold, tumbles into the sea, and never spoke more.

By this time the boatswain was dead, for as soon as Philmore saw the master laid hold of, he raised up the axe and divided his enemy's head in two.

This noise brought the Captain upon deck, whom Cheeseman greeted with the blow of a mallet which broke his jawbone, but did not knock him down. Harradine came in then with the carpenter's adze, but Sparks the gunner, interposing between him and Captain Phillips, Cheeseman trips up his heels, and flung him into the arms of Charles Ivymay, one of his consorts, who that instant threw him into the sea. And at the same time Harradine compassed his business with the

---

[5] **aft** – hind part of a ship

[6] **dram** – a serving of liquor

Captain aforesaid. Cheeseman lost no time, but from the deck jumps into the hold and was about to beat out the brains of Archer the quartermaster, when Harry Giles, a young lad, came down after him, and asked that his life might be spared as an evidence of their own innocence. (For, because Archer had all the spoil and plunder in his custody, if his life were spared it might appear that these tragic proceedings were not undertaken with any dishonest view of seizing or stealing the goods for themselves.) Giles' prudent advice prevailed, and Archer and three more were made prisoners and secured.

The work being done, they went about ship, altered the course from Newfoundland to Boston, and arrived safe the 3rd of May following, to the great joy of that province.

On the 12th of May, 1724, a special Court of Admiralty was held for the trial of these pirates, when John Philmore, Edward Cheeseman, John Combs, Henry Giles, Charles Ivymay, John Bootman, and Henry Payne (the seven that joined together for the pirates' destruction) were honorably acquitted. And John Rose Archer, the quartermaster, William White, William Taylor, and William Phillips were condemned. The two last were reprieved for a year and a day in order to be recommended (though I don't know why) as objects of his Majesty's mercy. The two former were executed on the 2nd of June, and died very penitently.

At the place of execution Archer and White made the following declarations, with the assistance of two grave ministers that attended them.

The dying declarations of John Rose Archer and William White, on the day of their execution at Boston, June 2, 1724, for the crimes of Piracy.

First, the confession of Archer:

I greatly bewail my profaning of the Lord's Day, and my disobedience to my parents.

And I bewail my cursing and swearing, and my blaspheming the Name of the glorious God.

Unto these sins I have added the sins of unchastity. And I have provoked the Holy One, at length, to leave me unto the crimes of piracy and robbery; wherein, at last, I have brought myself under the guilt of murder also.

But one wickedness that has led me as much as any to all the rest, has been my beastly drunkenness. By strong drink I have been heated and hardened in the crimes that are now more bitter than death unto me.

I could wish that masters of vessels would not treat their men with so much severity as many of them do, which exposes them to great temptations.

And then the confession of White:

I am now, with sorrow, reaping the fruits of my disobedience to my parents, who used their endeavors to have me instructed in my Bible and my catechism.

And I am also reaping the fruits of my neglecting the public worship of God, and profaning the holy Sabbath.

And of my blaspheming the Name of God, my Maker.

But my drunkenness has had a great hand in bringing my ruin upon me. I was drunk when I was first enticed aboard the pirate ship.

And now, for all the vile things I did aboard, I confess the justice of God and man in what is done unto me.

The confession of both together:

We hope, we truly hate the sins whose burden lies so heavily upon our consciences.

We warn all people, *and particularly young people,* against such sins as these. We wish all may take warning by seeing us.

We beg for pardon, for the sake of Christ our Savior; and our hope is in Him alone. Oh, that in His blood our scarlet and crimson guilt may be all washed away!

We are conscious of a hard heart within us, full of wickedness. And we look upon God for His renewing grace upon us.

We bless God for the time of repentance which He has given us; and that He has not cut us off in the midst and height of our wickedness.

We are not without hope that God has been savingly at work upon our souls.

We are made conscious of our absolute need of the righteousness of Christ, that we may stand justified before God in that. We renounce all dependence on our own.

We are humbly thankful to the ministers of Christ for the great pains they have taken for our good. May the Lord reward their kindness.

We don't despair of mercy, but hope—through Christ—that when we die we shall find mercy with God and be received into His Kingdom.

We wish others, and especially the seafaring, may get good by what they see this day befalling us.

"How have I hated instruction,
and my heart despised reproof;
and have not obeyed the voice of my teachers,
nor inclined mine ear to them that instructed me!
I was almost in all evil
in the midst of the congregation and assembly."

— Proverbs 5:12-14

Chapter Eighteen

The Only Way of Escape

Like hungry lions, waves for sinners gape;
Leave then your sins behind, if you'll escape.

The waves of the sea are sometimes raised by God's command to be executioners of His threatenings upon sinners. When Jonah fled from the presence of the Lord to Tarshish, the text says, "The Lord sent out a great wind into the sea, and there was a mighty tempest, so that the ship was like to be broken" (Jonah 1:4). These were God's appointed officers to arrest the runaway prophet. And Psalm 148:8 tells us that the stormy winds fulfill His word. They fulfill not only His word of command in rising when God bids them, but His word of *threatening* also. And hence it is called "a destroying wind" (Jeremiah 51:1), and a stormy wind in God's fury (Ezekiel 13:13).

Application

If these be the executioners of the Lord's threatenings, how sad then is their condition that put forth to sea under the guilt of all their sins? O, if God should command the winds to go after and arrest you for all that you owe Him, where then would you be? How dare you set forth under the power of a divine threat, before

all be cleared between God and you? Sins in Scripture are called debts (Matthew 6:12). They are debts to God—not that we owe them to Him, or ought to sin, but are rather called debts because they render the sinner liable to God's judgments, even as debtors who owe a sum of money will suffer punishment if they do not have the ability to pay their debts. All sinners must suffer the curse, either in their own person (according to the express letter of the law: Genesis 2:17; Galatians 3:10) or their Surety, according to the implied intent of the law, revealed to be the mind of the Lawgiver (Genesis 3:15; Galatians 3:13-14).

Now he that by faith has an interest in this Surety, has his discharge sealed in the blood of Christ. All process at law, or from the law, is stopped (Romans 8:1). But if you are an unrepentant, persisting sinner, your debt remains upon your own score. And be sure your sin will find you out, wherever you go (Numbers 32:23).

If you continue in your sin, God's revenging hand for sin will be upon you. You may lose the sight and memory of your sins, but they will not lose sight of you. They follow hard after you—just as the hound chases the fleeting game upon the scent—until they catch you. And then consider how fearful a thing it is "to fall into the hands of the living God!" (Hebrews 10:31.) How quickly can a storm intercept you and bring you before the judgment seat of God!

Reflection

O my soul, what a case are you in, if this be true? Are not all your sins yet upon your own score? Have you not made light of Christ, and that precious blood of His, and have you not until now persisted in your rebellion against Him? And what can the end of this be at last, except ruin? There is abundant mercy indeed for returning sinners, but the gospel speaks of no mercy for persistent and unrepentant sinners. And though many who are going on in their sins are overtaken by grace, yet there is no grace promised to such as go on in sin. O, if God should arrest me by the next storm and call me to an account for all that I owe Him, I must then lie in the prison of hell for all eternity, for I can never pay the debt! Nay, all the angels in heaven cannot satisfy for it!

Being without Christ, I am under all the curses of the book of God, a child of Hagar. Lord, pity and spare me a little longer! O reveal Your

Christ unto me, and give me faith in His blood, and then You are fully satisfied at once, and I discharged for ever. O require not the debt at my hand, for then You will never be satisfied, nor I acquitted. What profit, Lord, is there in my blood?

  O my soul, make haste to this Christ, your City of Refuge! You know not how soon the avenger of blood may overtake you!

> Your sins are debts. God puts them to account.
> Can you tell, wretch, to what your debts amount?
> You fill the treasure of your sins each hour;
> Into His vials God pours out in power
> His righteous wrath, though now you see it not—
> But yet assure yourself, there's drop for drop.
>
> For every sand of patience running out
> A drop of wrath runs in. Soul, look about!
> God's treasure's almost full, as well as thine:
> When both are full, O then the dreadful time
> Of reck'ning comes. You shall not gain a day
> Of patience more. But see! There comes your way
> A messenger of Heav'n, upon the wing
> With his commission sealed to take and bring.
>
> You still reject Christ's offers? Well, next storm
> May be the messenger sent to perform
> This dreadful office. O then restless be,
> Till God in Christ be reconciled to thee.
>
> The sum is great, but if at Christ you get,
> Fear not: a Prince can pay a beggar's debt.
> Now, if the storm should rise, you need not fear;
> You're here, but yet the sinner is not there.
> A pardoned soul to sea may boldly go;
> He fears no judges, who does nothing owe.

A Concluding Appeal

I have now finished, and am looking to heaven for a blessing upon these weak labors. What use you will make of them, I know not. But this I know, that the day is coming when God will reckon with you for this, and all other helps and means given to you. And if these be not improved by you, be sure they shall be produced as a witness against you on that Day.

Readers, I beg you, in the name of Christ, before whom both you and I must shortly appear, that you receive not these things in vain. Did I know what other lawful means to use that might reach your hearts, they should not be in vain to you. But I cannot do God's part of the work, nor yours. Only I request you all, each and every one of you, into whose hands this shall come, that you will lay to heart what you read. Pray unto Him that holds the key of the house of David (that opens, and no man shuts), to open your hearts to receive to these truths. Alas! If you apply it not to yourselves, I have labored for nothing; the pen of the scribe is in vain. But God may make such an application of them, in one storm or another, as may make your hearts to tremble.

O reader! When death and eternity look you in the face, conscience may reflect upon these things to your horror and amazement, and make you cry out, "How have I hated knowledge, and my heart despised reproof! And have not obeyed the voice of my teachers, nor inclined my ears to them that instructed me!" (Proverbs 5:12-13.)

And O what a dreadful shriek will such souls give when the Lord opens their eyes to see that misery that they are here warned of! But if the Lord shall bless these writings to lead to your conversion, then we may say to you, as Moses did to Zebulun, the mariner's tribe, "Rejoice Zebulun, in thy going out" (Deuteronomy 33:18). The Lord will be with you wherever you turn yourselves. And, being in the bosom of the covenant, you are safe in the midst of all dangers.

O You who are the Father of spirits, who formed and can easily reform the heart, open the blind eye, unstop the deaf ear! Let the word take hold upon the heart! If You will but say the word, these weak labors shall prosper, to bring home many lost souls unto You! Amen.

— John Flavel

If you enjoyed *Pirates, Puritans, and the Perils of the High Seas,*
you may also enjoy:

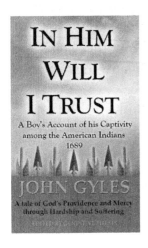

In Him Will I Trust:

A Boy's Account of his Captivity
among the American Indians

Without a Home
or Country:

A Gallant Tale
of the Last Stand
of the Confederacy,
by Cornelius Hunt,
One of her Officers

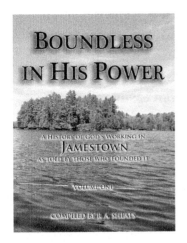

Boundless in His Power:

A History of
God's Working in Jamestown,
as told by those who founded it

John Paton
for Young Folks:

The classic Autobiography
of Missionary
John G. Paton

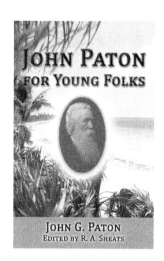

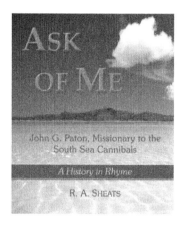

Ask of Me:

John G. Paton, Missionary
to the South Sea Cannibals,
a History in Rhyme

Makes a great family read-aloud!

Driven to Resistance:

The History of the
Revolutionary War,
as told by those who lived it

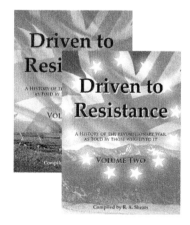

For a complete listing of available titles, please visit:
www.psalm78ministries.com

CPSIA information can be obtained
at www.ICGtesting.com
Printed in the USA
LVOW03s1055150116
470765LV00003B/4/P